An Evidence Based History of Reiki

An Evidence Based History of Reiki

A selection of articles
from *Reiki News Magazine*

International Center for Reiki Training

ISBN 1-886785-41-4

Published in the United States of America.

International Center for Reiki Training
21421 Hilltop St. #28, Southfield, MI 48033
Phone (800) 332-8112, (248) 948-8112 Fax (248) 948-9534
E-mail center@reiki.org   Website www.reiki.org

Table of Contents

Contributors

Hyakuten Inamoto

Hyakuten is from Kyoto, Japan and is a mendicant Buddhist monk, independent and nonsectarian. He is also a Reiki master who received his training in the original Japanese style from Mrs. Yamaguchi who learned directly from Dr. Hayashi. He is the founder of Komyo Reiki Kai. Contact him through his Website: www.komyo-reiki.jp/english/

William Lee Rand

William Lee Rand has received the Reiki master level of training from six Reiki masters including three from Japan. He has taught full time since 1989 and has practiced and taught in many countries around the world. He is founder and president of The International Center for Reiki Training, author of many Reiki books and is also publisher of the *Reiki News Magazine*

Marianne Streich

An Usui/Tibetan Reiki Master and Karuna Reiki® Master, Marianne practices and teaches Reiki in Seattle. Also a freelance editor and writer, she edits *Reiki News Magazine*, writes the column, "Getting the Most from Reiki," and is the author of *Reiki: A Guide for the Practice of Levels I and II*. Contact her through her website: www.reikiforliving.com.

The day will come when, after harnessing space, the winds, the tide, we shall harness for God the energies of love. And on that day, for the second time in the history of the world, we shall have discovered fire.

—Pierre Teilhard de Chardin

Usui Memorial Stone

An Evidence Based History of Reiki

BY WILLIAM LEE RAND

MY FIRST EXPERIENCE WITH metaphysical training was with the Rosicrucians. As a member, I received lessons in the form of monographs, which came in a packet with one to be read and followed each week. One of the things they said in the beginning is that you shouldn't believe something just because someone says it's true or because it's written in a book—that a person can say anything and a printing press will print anything, so you can't base your understanding of what is true on these criteria alone. They went on to say that the best way to learn about something is through experience and that this is especially true for metaphysical ideas and spiritual principles since the purpose of this type of knowledge isn't simply to understand the ideas or to enable you to have an intelligent conversation about them, but to actually use the information to improve your life and to help others. This really impressed me.

As the weeks went by, these monographs provided me with more thought provoking questions and new ways of thinking about things. One reading explained how important it is to always ask what a person's ideas are based on; where did they come from? Those who are clear thinkers and have done proper research on the topics they speak or write about will easily be able to answer this question. However, those who have only a casual understanding of the subject matter will not always have clear answers and will sometimes become upset that you are asking such a question. Yet this a valid enquiry and one should never hesitate to ask about it, especially if one is seeking a clear and deep understanding of the topic it covers. Otherwise all you might be getting is little more than rumors and hearsay, which is not useful in helping one decide what is true.

After you discover the origin of the ideas, it is important to think about the quality of the evidence. Does the author claim to be the only authority on the topic or to be the only one who has access to the source of the information, or, on the other hand, has the information been verified by other independent researchers through written records that anyone can access or through other verifiable sources? The rigorous collection and organization of evidence and the verification of the authenticity and veracity of information and its sources is the cornerstone of valid historical research.[1] This level of research takes time and effort and is not something that all authors are willing to do as it is much easier to simply repeat what others have said even though it may not be known whether the information has been verified by sufficient evidence.

Perhaps even more problematic than this aspect, and also one of the reasons why there is so much trouble in the world is that people have not been taught an effective method of determining what is real. Rather, in school, people are taught what the education system wants students to believe is real. Students aren't usually shown how to determine this for themselves. An exception to this is in some forms of higher education such as journalism classes and classes involving scientific research, where valid research methods are taught. But for the most part, the general public has not been taught the value of thinking in this more rigorous way. Because of this people often become conditioned to believe what they are told and because there are sometimes many versions of what is supposed to be real, they end up deciding to believe what everyone else in their peer group believes or what sounds good to them or what they want to believe is real. This is why it's possible for people to believe ideas for which there is very little meaningful evidence.

When researching a topic it is important to be as unbiased as possible and to be willing to give up an idea one has held if new, more accurate and verifiable information has been uncovered. This requires one to have a disciplined mind as some beliefs can be firmly held and therefore difficult to let go of, especially if they support one's personal philosophy and there is an emotional need for them to be true. Because of this, one's greatest allegiance must be to the highest standards of evidence and veracity concerning the facts of an issue, rather than the need to cling to and defend a previously held notion or belief. Those researchers with this level of commitment will abandon previously held understandings in favor of higher quality information when it is discovered. This level of research is important to use when we seek to understand the history of Reiki as increasingly more accurate information has been uncovered over time.

In the Reiki world there have been many attempts to accurately portray the history of Reiki. Unfortunately, only a few are based on evidence ascertained in the more complete manner I have previously described. The first history of Reiki we had in the West came from Mrs. Takata and while we honor her as the one who kept Reiki alive so that it could become popular the world over, the history of Reiki

[1] Charles Busha and Stephen P. Harter, *Research Methods in Librarianship: Techniques and Interpretations* (Academic Press: New York, NY, 1980).

she taught contained many details that have proven to be untrue. As an example, in her story of Reiki, she said that Usui Sensei had been the president of Doshisha University in Kyoto, Japan. When I became a Reiki Master in 1989, I was curious about any additional facts we might be able to learn about the founder. So, believing the story Takata told, I wrote a letter to Doshisha University asking about one of their presidents, Mikao Usui. I wanted to discover if they had any additional information about him that could add to our understanding of the kind of person he was. (And quite frankly I wondered why no one had done this previously.) They wrote me back explaining that they had done a very thorough search through all their records and could say quite certainly that he had never been the president of the university, nor had he been on the faculty or even enrolled as a student and that they knew nothing about him at all.[2] This information was very distressing to me. If one of the most central ideas in the story Takata told about the history of Reiki was false, then what other ideas were also false. This bothered me to the extent that I wondered if Takata had made up the whole thing including the idea of Reiki itself.

Further research has revealed that many additional ideas Takata included in her history of Reiki and in how she taught it have also proven to be untrue. She said that Usui Sensei had also attended the University of Chicago and received a degree in theology, that he had been a Christian and was seeking to discover how Jesus had healed when he discovered Reiki, that Reiki is an oral tradition and that the system of Reiki she taught was the unchanged system that had been taught by Usui Sensei.[3] Sadly these points have also proven to be false.

While I realized that we did not have a factual history of Reiki at that time, I also realized that the Reiki energy did heal and therefore was real. Because of this I decided that I would continue to practice and teach Reiki and keep looking for the historical facts.

One of the reasons that Reiki has historically been so difficult to research is due to the fact that when World War II ended and the Japanese were required to unconditionally surrender to the U.S., laws were enacted that banned all Eastern

[2] Some said that he might have used a different name or that the university records might have been lost during the war, but additional research included the examination of a list of all the presidents of Doshisha University, the periods of time they were president and biographies of each. There were no periods of time for which there was no president listed and none of the biographies were similar to that of the life of Mikao Usui. http://en.wikipedia.org/wiki/Doshisha_University. See page 14 and 15 for copies of the letters from Doshisha Universiity and the University of Chicago.

[3] *Mrs. Takata Speaks, The History of Reiki*, CD and transcript (Southfield, MI: Vision Publications, 1979).

healing methods and required that only Western medical methods be practiced. And while some of the Japanese healing groups such as the acupuncturists were able to continue practicing by creating a government licensing system, the members of the Usui Reiki Ryoho Gakkai[4] decided that they did not want to go through the process of licensing. So in order to continue practicing, they decided to become a secret society. After that they would only practice at their private meetings and would not talk about Reiki to others outside their group. Because of this, Reiki disappeared from view and was more or less forgotten about by almost everyone outside the group of Gakkai members.[5] Therefore, when people went to Japan and inquired about the system of Reiki started by Usui Sensei no one knew anything about it. Because of this, those who attempted to research Reiki in the '80s and early '90s were not successful.

Then in 1995, Toshitaka Mochizuki, a Japanese Reiki Master, wrote a book on Reiki that provided a few additional facts about the history such as an original version of the Usui Ideals. In 1997 *Reiki Fire* was published and it explained how the author, Arjava Petter and his wife Chetna Kobayashi had made contact with the then current president of the Usui Reiki Ryoho Gakkai, Mrs. Kimiko Koyama. The information in the book included the location of Usui Sensei's grave, and photos and a translation of the inscription on the memorial stone. This was the first book that contained meaningful information about the history of Reiki that was verifiable.

As soon as I found out about the book, I contacted Arjava Petter and he invited me to come to Japan. Laurelle Shanti Gaia and I went in September 1997, and Arjava took us to Mt. Kurama and to Mikao Usui's grave. I made two additional trips to Japan, in 1999 along with Walter Lubeck and Arjava Petter to do research for our book, *The Spirit of Reiki*, and in 2001 to take Reiki I&II from Mrs. Yamaguchi, who had learned Reiki directly from Hayashi Sensei. In 1999 and 2000 I sponsored Arjava and Chetna to come to the US to teach the Japanese Reiki Techniques workshops. It was through these books, workshops and events that verifiable information about the history of Reiki came to be known in the West. Since then additional pieces of the puzzle have been added.

The highest quality information about the history of Reiki comes from the Usui Reiki Ryoho Gakkai. This is based on the fact that the first president of the Gakkai was Usui Sensei and the following four presidents were all Shihans (Reiki

[4] This is the organization Usui Sensei started in April 1922 to practice and promote Reiki.

[5] Tadao Yamaguchi, *Light on the Origins of Reiki* (Twin Lakes, WI: Lotus Press, 2007), p. 66.

Masters) trained by Usui Sensei who are known to have the same knowledge and abilities as he had and were authorized to teach in his place when he was not present.[6] The following four presidents after Usui Sensei were Juzaburo Ushida, Kan'ichi Taketomi, Yoshibaru Watanabe and Hoichi Wanami.[7] Information from the Gakkai has come to us from Arjava Petter who had contact with Kimiko Koyama, the sixth president of the Gakkai and through Hiroshi Doi[8] who is a Gakkai member and has access to the Gakkai archives. Another important source of information is the writing of Tadao Yamaguchi, whose mother Chiyoko and many of his relatives learned Reiki from Hayashi Sensei.[9]

[6] See *Reiki News Magazine* (Spring 2011), p. 18 for a photo of Usui Sensei and all twenty Shihans he trained that includes a statement in the photo in Japanese indicating that each is authorized to teach in the same way as Usui Sensei. The exception is Wantanabe who received Okuden from Usui Sensei and was given Shinpiden from Ushida after Usui Sensei passed.

[7] Walter Lubeck, Frank Arjava Petter, William Lee Rand, *The Spirit of Reiki* (Twin Lakes, WI: Lotus Press, 2003), p. 17. This page contains a list of the presidents of the Gakkai and the fact that the first four had been trained by Usui Sensei.

[8] Hiroshi Doi, *Gendei Reiki-ho* (Southfield, MI: Vision Publications, 2013). Previously published but out of print; new addition available Fall 2013.

[9] Yamaguchi, *Origins of Reiki*.

December 17, 1991

Mr.William L.Rand
President
The Center for Spiritual Development
20782 Knobwoods Dr., Suite 203
Southfield, MI 48086 U.S.A.

Dear Mr.Rand:

First, you could get some informations on the history of Doshisha University from enclosed photocopies made from Doshisha University Catalogue and The Doshisha.
Second, I, aided by chief archivist, checked the mentioned person, Mikao Usui with the related documents in vain;List of graduate students on Doshisha Alumni Bulletin, Literatures relating to J.H.Neesima, and List of faculty and clerical members in those days. I just found out he was never the presidentof Doshisha. And the name never appeared, and neither left any traces on them.
So I am afraid I cannot provide you any information.

Sincerely,

Itsuro Nishida
Head, Public Services
Center for Academic Information
(formerly Library)
Doshisha University
Kyoto 602, Japan

THE UNIVERSITY OF CHICAGO
The Office of the University Registrar
CHICAGO, ILLINOIS 60637

November 9, 1990

William L. Rand
President
The Center for Spiritual Development
917 Woodcrest Drive
Royal Oak, MI 48067

Dear Mr. Rand:

In response to your recent correspondence our records do not indicate that Mikao Usui ever attended the University of Chicago.

I have enclosed our Announcements of the Divinity School.

Sincerely,

Maxine H. Sullivan
University Registrar

MHS/mn

History of Reiki

BY WILLIAM LEE RAND

From Left: Mikao Usui Sensei, Chujiro Hayashi and Hawayo Takata.
Takata photo taken June 11, 1979, Penticton, British Columbia, Canada. Used with permission from the estate of Gunter and Ursula Baylow.

The following referenced history of Reiki is taken from Reiki, The Healing Touch *and has been carefully researched to contain verified information from dependable sources.*

MRS. HAWAYO TAKATA (Takata Sensei) brought Reiki from Japan to the West in 1937 and continued to practice and teach until her passing in 1980. Because of her devotion, Reiki has been passed on to millions of people all over the world, and the numbers continue to grow! And as you will see, if it wasn't for her, Reiki most likely would never have been discovered by the West and even in Japan would have been practiced secretly by only a small number of people.

Until the 1990s, the only information we had about Reiki came from Takata Sensei. Her story of Reiki was recorded on tape, and this recording is still available along with a transcript of the contents.[1] In the past most people including many authors simply accepted Takata Sensei's interpretation of the history of Reiki as accurate without attempting to do any additional research. Because of this, her version of the story was repeated in all the earlier books written on Reiki. (Fortunately many current authors are using more recent historical information.)

[1] *Mrs. Takata Speaks, The History of Reiki,* (Southfield, MI: Vision Publications, 1979).

In the course of researching the origins of Reiki, I learned that Takata Sensei took liberties with the history of its development. In 1990, for example, I wrote to Doshisha University in Kyoto, Japan where Takata Sensei reported that the founder of Reiki, Usui Sensei, had held the office of president. I had hoped to gain additional information that would help us understand who Usui Sensei really was. I also contacted the University of Chicago, from which Usui Sensei had obtained a degree according to Takata Sensei. Neither university had ever heard of him.[2] This disappointing discovery led me to wonder if other parts of the Takata Sensei version of Reiki were also inaccurate. In talking with several early Reiki Masters about this discovery, I was told that Takata Sensei had westernized the story of Reiki by changing certain details and adding others to make it more appealing to Americans.

I continued to seek additional information about the history of Reiki, but attempts to secure it went slowly at first. The main reason for this is that after World War II, the U.S. government had complete control over Japan for a time and banned all Eastern healing methods in Japan and required that only Western medicine be practiced there. The members of the organization Usui Sensei started, the *Usui Reiki Ryoho Gakkai*, decided they wanted to find a way to continue to practice Reiki. Some of the other healing groups such as the Acupuncturists were able to get a license to practice, but the Gakkai chose not to go through this process. In order to continue to practice Reiki, they decided to become a secret society and practice only among themselves and not talk about Reiki to anyone outside their organization.[3] This made it difficult for anyone to learn about Reiki including the Japanese. In fact, if someone in Japan wanted to learn Reiki after the war, he or she had to travel to the U.S. to learn or had to learn from a Western trained Reiki teacher who traveled to Japan. Because of this, even now most Reiki practiced in Japan is a combination of Western and Japanese Reiki.

This is why an accurate history of Reiki took so long to unfold up to that point in time. Then in 1996, I received from Japan a copy of the Original Reiki Ideals, which were different and more expansive than what had been presented by Mrs. Takata. They included the idea that chanting and offering prayers are important to Reiki practice.[4] In 1997, Arjava Petter's book, *Reiki Fire* was published, which was the first of a series of books on Japanese Reiki. He along with

[2] See http://www.reiki.org/Download/TakataLettersAnd Documents.pdf

[3] Tadao Yamaguchi, *Light on the Origins of Reiki* (Twin Lakes, WI: Lotus Press, 2007), p. 66.

[4] Toshitaka Mochizuki, *Iyashi No Te [Healing Hands]* (1995), p. 227, ISBN 4-88481-420-7 C0011 P1400E; "The Original Reiki Ideals," *Reiki News* (Fall 1996). To order the "Original Reiki Ideals": www.reikiwebstore.com.

his wife, Chetna Kobayashi, had made contact with the Gakkai. They had discovered the location of Usui Sensei's grave and many other facts including information on the Japanese Reiki Techniques, all of which were revealed in his books and subsequent workshops.

Invited by Arjava Petter, Laura Gifford (now Laurelle Gaia) and I went to Japan in 1997, and with Arjava as our guide, we were taken to Usui Sensei's grave and Mt. Kurama and much of the new information was explained to us.[5]

In 1999 and 2000 I invited Arjava and Chetna to come to teach workshops on the Japanese Reiki Techniques across the United States. In addition, in November, 2001, I took Reiki I&II from Chiyoko Yamaguchi in Japan, a Shihan (Reiki Master) who received her training from Hayashi Sensei. (She passed on in 2003). In October 2002 I took Gendai Reiki training from Hiroshi Doi—who is a member of the *Usui Reiki Ryoho Gakkai*—and also had two detailed interviews with him.[6] It is from these sources and my continued contact with these and other Reiki researchers that my understanding of the history of Reiki along with how Usui Sensei and Hayashi Sensei taught and practiced Reiki has developed.

A More Accurate History of Reiki

The following is an updated history of Reiki based on accurate, verifiable information. Where possible, sources have been referenced so others can follow up on this research if desired. The history begins with a look at the inscription on the memorial stone that was erected in 1927 in memory of Mikao Usui Sensei, founder of the Reiki healing system.

The Inscription on the Usui Memorial

The inscription on the Usui Memorial, dating from 1927, was written by Juzaburo Ushida, a Shihan who was trained by Usui Sensei and able to teach and practice Reiki the same way he did.[7] He also succeeded Usui Sensei as president

[5] For more information, see Appendix A, "Discovering the Roots of Reiki," and The Inscription on the Usui Memorial section below.

[6] William Lee Rand, "An Interview with Hiroshi Doi," *Reiki News Magazine*, Pts. 1 and 2 (Summer 2003), p. 9-11; (Fall 2003), p. 12-14. Also see p. 69 in this book.

[7] Tadao Yamaguchi. "Excerpts from Light on the Origin of Reiki" *Reiki News Magazine* (Spring 2011), p. 19. Included in this article is a photo of the 20 shihan taught by Usui Sensei. The text below the photo indicates that these are the students of Usui Sensei who are authorized to teach in the same way he taught. Juzaburo Ushida is in the photo.

of the Usui Reiki Ryoho Gakkai. Masayuki Okata, also a member of the Usui Reiki Ryoho Gakkai, was the editor. The English translation was done by Tetsuyuki Ono and is reprinted here from the book, *Iyashino Gendai Reiki- ho*, with permission from the author, Hiroshi Doi.

The large kanji at the top of the memorial stone reads: "Memorial of Usui Sensei's Virtue." The remainder of the inscription reads as follows:

What you can naturally realize through cultivation and training is called "VIRTUE" and it is called "MERIT" to spread a method of leadership and relief and practice it. It is people of many merits and a good deal of virtue that can be eventually called a great founder. People who started a new learning and founded a fresh sect among sages, philosophers, geniuses etc., named from the ancient times, were all those as mentioned above. We can say that Usui-Sensei is also one of those people.

He started newly a method to improve body and spirit based on REIKI in the universe. Hearing of the rumor, people who would like to learn the treatment and undergo the cure gathered from all quarters all at once. Really, it was very busy indeed.

Usui-Sensei, whose popular name is Mikao and whose pen name is Gyohan, came from Taniai-village, Yamagata- district, Cifu Prefecture, and had forefathers named Tsunetane Chiba who had played an active part as a military commander between the end of Heian Period and the beginning of Kamakura Period (1180-1230). His father's real name is Taneuji and his popular name is Uzaemon. His mother came and got married from the family named Kawai.

Usui-Sensei was born on 15th August, 1865. Having learned under difficulties in his childhood, he studied hard with efforts and he was by far superior in ability to his friends.

After growing up, he went over to Europe and America, and also studied in China. In spite of his real ability, however, he was not always successful in life. Although he was compelled to lead an unfortunate and poor life so often, he strove much more than before to harden his body and mind without flinching from the difficulties.

One day, Usui-Sensei climbed Mt. Kurama, where he began to do penance while fasting. Suddenly on the twenty first day from the start, he felt a great REIKI over his head, and at the same time as he was spiritually awakened he acquired the REIKI cure. When he tried it on his own body and members' of his family also, it brought an immediate result on them.

Having said "It is much better to give this power widely to a lot of people in the world and enjoy it among them than to keep it exclusively by his family members," Usui-Sensei moved his dwelling to Aoyama Harajuku, Tokyo in April, 1922 and established an institute, where the REIKI cure was instructed openly to the public and the treatment was given, too. People came there from far and near to ask for his guidance and cure, and they over-flowed outside, making a long line.

Tokyo had a very big fire caused by a great earthquake in Kanto district in September, 1923, when the injured and sick persons suffered from pains everywhere. Usui-Sensei felt a deep anxiety about that, and he was engaged in a cure, going around inside the city every day. We can hardly calculate how many persons were saved from death with his devotion. His activities of relief, in which he extended his hands of love over to those suffering people against this emergent situation, can be outlined as noted above.

Thereafter, his training center became too small to receive the visitors, so he built a new house in Nakano outside the city in February 1925 and transferred there. As his reputation got higher and higher, it was so often when he received an offer of engagement from everywhere throughout the nation. In accordance with these requests he traveled to Kure and Hiroshima, then entered Saga and reached Fukuyama. It was at the inn at which he stayed on his way that he caught a disease abruptly, and he passed away at the age of sixty-two.

His wife got married, coming from the Suzuki family, and she is named Sadako and has a son and a daughter. The son's name is Fuji, and he succeeds to the Usui family.

Usui-Sensei's natural character was gentle and prudent, and he did not keep up appearances. His body was big and sturdy, and his face was always beaming with a smile. But when he faced the difficulties he went ahead with a definite will and yet persevered well, keeping extremely careful. He was a man of versatile talents and also a book lover, knowing well in the wide range from history, biography, medical science, canons of Christianity and Buddhism and psychology up to magic of fairyland, art of curse, science of divination and physiognomy.

In my opinion, it is evident to everybody that Usui-Sensei's cultivation & training were based on his career of art and science, and the cultivation & training became a clue to create the REIKI cure.

Reviewing the fact, I understand what the REIKI cure is aiming at is not only to heal the diseases but also to correct the mind by virtue of a God-sent spiritual ability, keep the body healthy and enjoy a welfare of life. In teaching the persons, therefore, we are supposed to first let them realize the last instructions of the Emperor Meiji, and chant the 5 admonitions morning and evening to keep them in mind.

The 5 admonitions in question are:

1. Don't get angry today.
2. Don't be grievous.

3. Express your thanks.
4. Be diligent in your business.
5. Be kind to others.

These are really the important precepts for a cultivation, just the same as those by which the ancient sages admonished themselves. Usui-Sensei emphasized that 'This is surely a secret process to bring a good fortune and also a miraculous medicine to remedy all kinds of diseases,' by which he made his purpose of teaching clear and accurate. Furthermore, he tried to aim at making his way of guidance as easy and simple as possible, so nothing is difficult to understand therein. Every time when you sit quietly and join your hands to pray and chant morning and evening, you can develop a pure and sound mind, and there is just an essence in making the most of that for your daily life. This is the reason why the REIKI cure can very easily spread over anybody.

The phase of life is very changeable in these days, and people's thoughts are apt to change, too. Could we fortunately succeed in spreading the REIKI cure everywhere, we feel sure that it would have to be very helpful in order to prevent people from disordering their moral sense. It never extends people anything but the benefits of healing long term illness, chronic disease and bad habit.

The number of pupils who learned from Usui-Sensei amounts to more than 2000 persons. Some leading pupils living in Tokyo among them gather at the training center and take over his work, while other pupils in the country also do everything to popularize the REIKI cure. Although our teacher already passed away, we have to do the very best to hand the REIKI cure down to the public forever and spread it much more. Ah! What a great thing he did; to have unsparingly given people what he had felt and realized by himself!

As a result of our pupils' recent meeting and discussion, we decided to erect a stone monument at the graveyard in his family temple so that we may bring his virtuous deed to light and transmit it to posterity; so, I was requested to arrange an epitaph for the monument. As I was much impressed by his great meritorious deed and also struck by our pupils' warm hearts of making much of the bond between master and pupil, I dared not refuse the request, but described the outline.

Therefore, I do expect heartily that people in the future generations would not forget to look up at the monument in open-eyed wonder.

—Usuida, in February, 1927. Edited by Masayuki Okada, The Junior 3rd Rank, the 3rd Order of Merit, Doctor of Literature. Written by Juzaburo Usuhida, The Junior 4th Class of Services, Rear Admiral.

Mikao Usui

Mikao Usui, or Usui Sensei as he is called by Reiki students in Japan, was born August 15, 1865 in the village of Taniai in the Yamagata district of Gifu prefecture, which is located near present-day Nagoya, Japan.[8]

He had an avid interest in learning and worked hard at his studies. As he grew older, he traveled to Europe and China to further his education. His curriculum included medicine, psychology and religion as well as the art of divination, which Asians have long considered to be a worthy skill.[9] Usui Sensei also became a member of the Rei Jyutu Ka, a metaphysical group dedicated to developing psychic abilities.[10] He had many jobs including civil servant, company employee and journalist, and he helped rehabilitate prisoners.[11] Eventually he became the secretary to Shinpei Goto, head of the department of health and welfare who later became the mayor of Tokyo. The connections Usui Sensei made at this job helped him to also become a successful businessman.[12]

The depth and breadth of his experiences inspired him to direct his attention toward discovering the purpose of life. In his search he came across the description of a special state of consciousness that once achieved would not only provide an understanding of one's life purpose, but would also guide one to achieve it. This special state is called An-shin Ritus-mei (pronounced on sheen dit sue may). In this special state, one is always at peace regardless of what is taking place in the outer world. And it is from this place of peace that one completes one's life purpose. One of the special features of this state is that it maintains itself without any effort on the part of the individual; the experience of peace simply wells up spontaneously from within and is a type of enlightenment.

[8] Inscription on Usui Memorial, Saihoji Temple, Suginami, Tokyo, Japan.

[9] Inscription on Usui Memorial.

[10] Mochizuki, *Iyashi No Te*. See note 3.

[11] Yamaguchi, *Light on the Origins of Reiki*, p. 61.

[12] "Searching the Roots of Reiki," *The Twilight Zone* (April 1986),: p. 140-143. This article can be viewed on the web at http://www.pwpm.com/threshold/origins2.html. (Note that this Japanese magazine is no longer in business.)

Usui Sensei understood this concept on an intellectual level and dedicated his life to achieving it; this is considered to be an important step on Usui Sensei's spiritual path. He discovered that one path to An-shin Ritsu-mei is through the practice of Zazen meditation. So he found a Zen teacher who accepted him as a student and began to practice Zazen. After three years practice, he had not been successful and sought further guidance. His teacher suggested a more severe practice in which the student must be willing to die in order to achieve An-shin Ritsu-mei.[13,14]

So with this in mind he prepared for death and in February, 1922, he went to Mt. Kurama to fast and meditate until he passed to the next world. In addition, we know there is a small waterfall on Mt. Kurama where even today people go to meditate. This meditation involves standing under the waterfall and allowing the water to strike and flow over the top of the head, a practice that is said to activate the crown chakra. Japanese Reiki Masters think that Usui Sensei may have used this meditation as part of his practice. In any case, as time passed he became weaker and weaker. It was now March, 1922 and at midnight of the twenty-first day, a powerful light suddenly entered his mind through the top of his head and he felt as if he had been struck by lightning; this caused him to fall unconscious.

As the sun rose, he awoke and realized that whereas before he had felt very weak and near death, he was now filled with an extremely enjoyable state of vitality that he had never experienced before; a miraculous type of high frequency spiritual energy had displaced his normal consciousness and replaced it with an amazingly new level of awareness. He experienced himself as being the energy and consciousness of the Universe and that the special state of enlightenment he had sought had been given to him as a gift. He was overjoyed by this realization.

When this happened, he was filled with excitement and went running down the mountain. On his way down he stubbed his toe on a rock and fell down. And in the same way anyone would do, he placed his hands over the toe, which was in pain. As he did this, healing energy began flowing from his hands all by itself.

[13] Frank Arjava Petter, *This is Reiki: Transformation of Body, Mind and Soul, From the Origins to the Practice* (Twin Lakes: WI: Lotus Press) p. 44.

[14] In an alternate version of this story it is said that Usui Sensei's personal life and business had failed and that he had gone to Mt. Kurama to meditate to gain clarity on what to do to solve his problems. See Takai, "Searching the Roots of Reiki," p. 140-143.

The pain in his toe went away and the toe was healed. Usui Sensei was amazed by this. He realized that in addition to the illuminating experience he had received, he had also received the gift of healing.[15]

Usui Sensei practiced this new ability with his family and developed his healing system through experimentation and by using skills and information based on his previous study of religious practices, philosophy and spiritual disciplines. He called his system of healing Shin-Shin Kai-Zen Usui Reiki Ryo-Ho (The Usui Reiki Treatment Method for Improvement of Body and Mind)[16] or in its simplified form Usui Reiki Ryoho (Usui Reiki Healing Method). It is important to know that Usui Sensei didn't create Reiki as there were other methods of Reiki healing in Japan prior to Usui Sensei creating his method and in fact one was called Reiki Ryoho.[17]

In April 1922, he moved to Tokyo and started a healing society that he named Usui Reiki Ryoho Gakkai (Usui Reiki Healing Method Society). He also opened a Reiki clinic in Harajuku, Aoyama, Tokyo. There he taught classes and gave treatments.[18]

The first degree of his training was called Shoden (First Degree) and was divided into four levels: Loku-Tou, Go-Tou, Yon-Tou, and San-Tou. (Note that when Takata Sensei taught this level, which in the West we refer to as Reiki Level I, she combined all four levels into one. This is most likely why she did four attunements for Level I.) The next degree was called Okuden (Inner Teaching) and had two levels: Okuden-Zen-ki (first part), and Okuden-Koe-ki (second part). The next degree was called Shinpiden (Mystery Teaching), which is what Western Reiki calls Master level. The Shinpiden level includes, Shihan-Kaku (assistant teacher) and Shihan (venerable teacher).[19]

Contrary to previous understanding, Usui Sensei had only three symbols, the same three we use in the West in Reiki II. He did not use a master symbol. This

[15] Doi, *Iyashino Gendai Reiki-ho, Modern Reiki Method of Healing*, p. 35. This story has been passed down within the Usui Reiki Ryoho Gakkai. According to Doi, it is also written in "Kaiin no tame no Reiki Ryoho no Shiori" (Guide of Reiki Ryoho for the members), September 1, 1974.

[16] This is based on the translation of an original document written by Usui Sensei. See: http://www.reiki.org/japanesetechniques/5principles.html

[17] William Lee Rand, "Reiki Before Usui," *Reiki News Magazine* (Spring 2014), p. 32-33. Also see p. 39 in this book.

[18] Yamaguchi, *Light on the Origins of Reiki*, p. 63-64.

[19] Walter Lubeck, Frank Arjava Petter, William Lee Rand, *The Spirit of Reiki* (Twin Lakes, WI: Lotus Press, 2003).

fact has been verified by Hiroshi Doi and by research done by Hyakuten Inamoto, Arjava Petter and Tadao Yamaguchi.[20]

In 1923, the great Kanto earthquake devastated Tokyo. More than 140,000 people died and over half of the houses and buildings were shaken down or burned. An overwhelming number of people were left homeless, injured, sick and grieving.[21] Usui Sensei felt great compassion for the people and began treating as many as he could with Reiki. This was a tremendous amount of work, and it was at this time that he began training other Shihan (teachers) so that they could help him more quickly train others to be Reiki practitioners and help the sick and injured. It was also at this time that he further developed his system of Reiki, including adding the three symbols and devising a more formal Reiju (attunement) process.[22]

The Reiju process was different than the method used now in that Usui Sensei had just one type of Reiju that was given over and over. He didn't have a different Reiju for each level and there was no Reiju to activate the symbols. It was taught that it is important for the student to get as many Reiju as possible as this was an important way to increase and refine the quality of one's Reiki energy.[23]

Demand for Reiki became so great that he outgrew his clinic, so in 1925 he built a bigger one in Nakano, Tokyo. Because of this, Usui Sensei's reputation as a healer spread all over Japan. He began to travel so he could teach and treat more people. During his travels across Japan he directly taught more than 2,000 students and initiated twenty Shihan,[24] each being given the same understanding of Reiki and approved to teach and give Reiju in the same way he did.[25]

[20] William Lee Rand, "Interview With Hiroshi Doi Sensei, Part I," *Reiki News Magazine* (Spring 2014) p. 27. Also see p. 55 in this book. Frank Arjava Petter, *This is Reiki* (Twin Lakes, WI: Lotus Press, 2012), p. 174

[21] "Earthquakes Tokyo-Yokohama," *Encyclopedia Britannica* (1997), CD-ROM.

[22] Frank Arjava Petter, *Reiki Darma Newsletter* Number 31, January 1, 2011

[23] William Lee Rand, "Interview With Hiroshi Doi Sensei, Part I" *Reiki News Magazine* (Spring 2014), p. 27. Also see p. 55 in this book.

[24] Go to *Reiki News Magazine* (Spring 2011), p. 18 for a photo of Usui Sensei and the twenty Shihan. Note that while all in the photo were authorized to give Reiju, some were not Shinpiden. In those days some of the centers did not have a Shinpiden to give Reiju so Reiju was taught to the leader of the center.

[25] Yamaguchi, *Light on the Origins of Reiki*, p. 63-64.

The Japanese government issued him a *Kun San To* award for doing honorable work to help others.[26] While traveling to Fukuyama to teach, he suffered a stroke and died March 9, 1926.[27] His grave is at Saihoji Temple, in Suginami, Tokyo, although some claim that his ashes are located elsewhere.

After Usui Sensei died, his students erected a memorial stone next to his gravestone. (See page 8.) Mr. J. Ushida, a Shihan trained by Usui Sensei, took over as president of the Usui Reiki Ryoho Gakkai, and was responsible for creating and erecting the Usui Memorial stone and ensuring that the gravesite would be maintained. Mr. Ushida was followed by Mr. Ilichi Taketomi, Mr. Yoshiharu Watanabe, Mr. Toyoichi Wanami and Ms. Kimiko Koyama. The current successor to Usui Sensei is Mr. Mahayoshi Kondo, who became president in 1998.

Contrary to what we have been told in the West, there is no "lineage bearer" or "Grand Master" of the organization started by Usui Sensei—only the succession of presidents listed above.[28] Among the twenty teachers initiated by Usui Sensei are Toshihiro Eguchi, Jusaburo Guida, Kan'ichi Taketomi, Toyoichi Wanami, Yoshiharu Watanabe, Keizo Ogawa, J. Ushida, and Chujiro Hayashi.[29] Contrary to one version of the Reiki story, Chujiro Hayashi was not the Gakkai's successor to Usui Sensei, but rather Mr. J. Ushida as previously mentioned. It is also important to note that the first four presidents of the Gakkai who followed Usui Sensei were Shihan who had been trained directly by Usui Sensei, thus assuring that the Gakkai understanding, practice and teaching methods were the same as that of Usui Sensei.

Chujiro Hayashi

Before his passing, Usui Sensei had asked Hayashi Sensei to open his own Reiki clinic and to expand and develop Reiki Ryoho based on his previous experience as a medical doctor in the Navy. Motivated by this request, Hayashi Sensei started a school and clinic called *Hayashi Reiki Kenkyukai* (Institute). After Usui Sensei's passing he left the Gakkai.[30]

[26] Takai, *The Twilight Zone*, p. 140-143.

[27] Inscription on Usui Memorial.

[28] Frank Arjava Petter, *Reiki Fire*, (Twin Lakes, WI: Lotus Light, 1997), p. 26. ISBN 0-914955-50-0.

[29] This list comes from the research of Frank Arjava Petter.

[30] William Lee Rand, "An Interview with Hiroshi Doi, Part II," *Reiki News Magazine*, (Fall 2003), p. 12. Also see p. 75 in this book.

At his clinic he kept careful records of all the illnesses and conditions patients who came to see him had. He also kept records of which Reiki hand positions worked best to treat each patient. Based on these records he created the *Reiki Ryoho Shinshin* (Guidelines for Reiki Healing Method).[31] This healing guide was part of a class manual he gave to his students. Many of his students received their Reiki training in return for working in his clinic.[32]

Hayashi Sensei also changed the way Reiki sessions are given. Rather than have the client seated in a chair and treated by one practitioner as Usui Sensei had done, Hayashi Sensei had the client lie on a treatment table and receive treatment from several practitioners at a time. He also created a new more effective system for giving Reiju (attunements).[33] In addition, he developed a new method of teaching Reiki that he used when he traveled. In this method, he taught both Shoden and Okuden (Reiki I&II) together in one five-day seminar. Each day included two to three hours of instruction and one Reiju.[34]

Because of his trip to Hawaii in 1937–38 prior to the Japanese attack on Pearl Harbor, he was asked by the Japanese military to provide information about the location of warehouses and other military targets in Honolulu. He refused to do so and was declared a traitor. This caused him to "lose face," which meant he and his family would be disgraced and would be ostracized from Japanese society. The only solution was seppuku (ritual suicide), which he carried out. He died honorably on May 11, 1940.[35]

Hawayo Takata

The following is a summary of Mrs. Hawayo Takata's version of her early years leading up to her contact with Reiki at the Hayashi clinic:

She stated that she was born on December 24th, 1900, on the island of Kauai, Hawaii. Her parents

[31] A translation of this healing guide can be found on p. 63 of *Reiki The Healing Touch*.

[32] Frank Arjava Petter interviewing Tsutomo Oishi, a member of Usui Reiki Ryoho Gakkai.

[33] Rand, "An Interview with Hiroshi Doi, Part II," *Reiki News Magazine*, (Fall 2003), p. 12. Also see p. 75 in this book.

[34] Yamaguchi, *Light on the Origins of Reiki*, p. 28.

[35] Ibid., p. 69.

were Japanese immigrants and her father worked in the sugar cane fields. She eventually married the bookkeeper of the plantation where she was employed. His name was Saichi Takata and they had two daughters. In October 1930 Saichi died at the age of 34, leaving Mrs. Takata to raise their two children.

In order to provide for her family, she had to work very hard with little rest. After five years she developed severe abdominal pain and a lung condition, and she had a nervous breakdown. Soon after this one of her sisters died and it was Mrs. Takata's responsibility to travel to Japan, where her parents had resettled to deliver the news. She also felt she could receive help for her health in Japan.

After informing her parents, she entered a hospital and stated that she was diagnosed with a tumor, gallstones, appendicitis and asthma.[36] *She was told to prepare for an operation but opted to visit Hayashi Sensei's clinic instead.*

Mrs. Takata was unfamiliar with Reiki but was impressed that the diagnosis of Reiki practitioners at the clinic closely matched the doctor's at the hospital. She began receiving treatments. Two Reiki practitioners would treat her each day. The heat from their hands was so strong, she said, that she thought they were secretly using some kind of equipment. Seeing the large sleeves of the Japanese kimono worn by one, she thought she had found the secret place of concealment. Grabbing his sleeves one day she startled the practitioner, but, of course, found nothing. When she explained what she was doing, he began to laugh and then told her about Reiki and how it worked.

Mrs. Takata got progressively better and in four months was completely healed. She wanted to learn Reiki for herself. In the spring of 1936 she received First Degree Reiki from Dr. Hayashi. She then worked with him for a year and received Second Degree Reiki. Mrs. Takata returned to Hawaii in 1937, followed shortly thereafter by Hayashi Sensei and his daughter who came to help establish Reiki there. In February of 1938 Hayashi Sensei initiated Hawayo Takata as a Reiki Master.

To summarize Takata Sensei's Reiki background, she traveled from Hawaii to Japan to tell her parents about the death of her sister. Having been diagnosed with several ailments, the main one being asthma, she was guided to Hayashi Sensei's clinic in Tokyo and after receiving four months of Reiki treatments was completely cured.[37] She wanted to learn Reiki in order to continue treating herself and also to take it back to Hawaii to share with others. Hayashi Sensei allowed her to work at his clinic and also began giving her Reiki training. She

[36] Vera Graham, "Mrs. Takata Opens Minds to Reiki," *The (San Mateo) Times*, May 17, 1975.

[37] Patsy Matsura, "Mrs. Takata and Reiki Power," *Honolulu Advertiser*, Feb. 25, 1974.

worked one year at the clinic and eventually received the *Shinpiden* level (Reiki Master). Hayashi Sensei officially acknowledged this in Hawaii on February 21, 1938, and also stated that she was one of thirteen Reiki Masters trained by him.[38]

Takata Sensei practiced Reiki in Hawaii, establishing several clinics, one of which was located in Hilo on the Big Island. She gave treatments and initiated students up to Reiki II. She became a well-known healer and traveled to the U.S. mainland and other parts of the world teaching and giving treatments. She was a powerful healer who attributed her success to the fact that she did a lot of Reiki on each client. She would often do multiple treatments, each sometimes lasting hours, and she often initiated members of a client's family so they could give Reiki to the client as well.

It was not until after 1970 that Takata Sensei began initiating Reiki Masters. She charged a fee of $10,000 for Mastership even though the training took only a weekend.[39] This high fee was not part of the Usui system, and she may have charged this fee as her way of creating a feeling of respect for Reiki. She said that one should never do treatments or provide training for free, but should always charge a fee or get something in return. She also said that one must study with just one Reiki teacher and stay with that teacher the rest of one's life.[40] In addition, she said that she did not provide written instruction or allow her students to take notes or to tape record the classes and students were not allowed to make any written copies of the Reiki symbols. She said that this was because Reiki is an oral tradition and that everything had to be memorized.[41] While this is generally true, she didn't always teach the same way and in at least one class she allowed her students to take notes and gave them handouts.[42]

It is not certain why she said Reiki is an oral tradition or why she taught Reiki this way. What we do know from our research in Japan and the research of others is that these rules are not part of the way Usui Sensei or Hayashi Sensei prac-

[38] This information was recorded on Mrs. Takata's Reiki certificate and in Mrs. Takata's handwritten notes dated May 1936. A copy of her Reiki certificate is included in the article "How Hawayo Takata Practiced and Taught Reiki" located on page 86.

[39] Bethel Phaigh, "Journey into Consciousness," p. 130. Other Masters initiated by Mrs. Takata have confirmed that she gave Reiki Master training in a weekend.

[40] We know that Keizo Ogawa took Reiki Master training from Usui Sensei and Kan'ichi Taketomi, so it is not likely this rule came from Usui Sensei.

[41] "Mrs. Takata Speaks." See footnote 1. This was also explained to me by Bethal Phaigh in 1981 when I took Reiki I from her.

[42] William Lee Rand, "Takata's Handouts," *Reiki News Magazine* (Summer 2009): p. 58. This article contains the handouts and notes taken during one of her classes.

ticed Reiki. In fact, Takata Sensei received a Reiki manual from Hayashi Sensei indicating that the oral tradition was not how Hayashi Sensei taught.[43] In addition, Takata Sensei taught Reiki differently from how she had been taught. She simplified and standardized the hand positions so that every treatment would be the same. She called this the "foundation treatment," containing just eight hand positions.[44] She also eliminated the Japanese Reiki Techniques.

It is also likely that she is the one who changed the attunement process by creating a different attunement for each level, indicated that the attunement empowered the symbols and added the Master symbol, as these features were not taught by either Usui Sensei or Hayashi Sensei.[45]

Before Mrs. Takata made her transition on December 11, 1980, she had initiated twenty-two Reiki Masters.[46] These twenty-two Masters began teaching others. However, Mrs. Takata had made each one take a sacred oath to teach Reiki exactly as she had taught. This made it difficult for most of them to change, even though some of her rules made it more difficult to learn, which seemed to go against the nature of Reiki.

This version of the history of Reiki from Usui Sensei to Mrs. Takata relies on verifiable information that has taken a long time to reach the West. In addition to the reasons for this mentioned earlier, there are a number of others. After Hayashi Sensei died and World War II ended, Takata Sensei stated that all the other Reiki Masters in Japan had died during the war and that she was the only Reiki Master in the world.[47] Therefore, most people refrained from researching

[43] A translation of this manual is on p. 63 of *Reiki The Healing Touch.*

[44] John Harvey Gray and Lourdes Gray with Steven McFadden and Elisabeth Clark, *Hand to Hand, The Longest-Practicing Reiki Master Tells His Story* (Gray, 2002), p. 93.

[45] Rand, "Origin of the Usui Reiki Master Symbol," *Reiki News Magazine* (Spring 2014): p. 34-35. Also see p. 82 in this book.

[46] Before she died, Takata Sensei created a list of the twenty-two Masters she had initiated. They are: George Araki (deceased), Dorothy Baba (deceased), Ursula Baylow (deceased), Rick Bockner, Barbara Brown (deceased), Fran Brown (deceased), Patricia Ewing, Phyllis Lei Furumoto, Beth Gray (deceased), John Gray (deceased), Iris Ishikura (deceased), Harry Kuboi, Ethel Lombardi (deceased), Barbara McCullough (deceased), Mary McFadyen, Paul Mitchell, Bethel Phaigh (deceased), Barbara Weber Ray, Shinobu Saito, Kay Yamashita (Mrs. Takata's sister), Virginia Samdahl (deceased), and Wanja Twan.

[47] Graham, "Mrs. Takata Opens Minds to Reiki." This is also stated on her Reiki flyers dated July 1975 and June 1976.

the history of Reiki, thinking she was the only authority. Many of the Masters she initiated also discouraged people from doing such research, stating that it was not needed, as their knowledge of Reiki was complete. Add to all this the fact that the Gakkai had become a secret society along with the linguistic, cultural, and geographic barriers that separated the United States from Japan, and it is easy to see why most authors simply accepted her story as true without seeking verification. Most did not realize that the organization started by Usui Sensei still existed in Japan and that contact with them, while difficult, was still possible.

Reiki since Mrs. Takata

Reiki energy is very flexible and creative, treating each unique situation with a unique response and working freely with all other forms of healing. The Reiki energy itself provides a wonderful model for the practice of Reiki. This began to be acknowledged gradually after Takata Sensei passed on. In the mid-1980s, Iris Ishikura, one of Takata's Masters, trained two Reiki Masters at a more reasonable fee and made them promise they would also charge a reasonable fee. The Masters trained by Ishikura at this lower fee began training many other Masters in turn. Out of this group, many were open to change and began allowing the wisdom of the Reiki energy to guide them in the way they should practice and teach Reiki. Because of this, restrictive rules began to fall away. Reiki classes became more open and more supportive of the learning process. Workbooks were created, notes and tape recordings were allowed, reasonable fees were charged, and many began studying with more than one teacher. All this generated greater respect for Reiki. It also increased people's understanding of Reiki and improved their healing skills. With lower fees, the practice of Reiki began to grow quickly and spread all over the world. It is estimated that there are at least 1,000,000 Reiki Masters in the world today with well over 4,000,000 practitioners, and the numbers continue to grow!

Excerpt from the Reiki Ryoho Hikkei

TRANSLATED BY HYAKUTEN INAMOTO

Editor's note: The following is a translation of the first two sections from the Reiki workbook that Usui sensei gave to his Reiki students. Reiki Ryoho Hikkei is translated to mean Reiki Healing Art Handbook. The sections that follow are Usui Reiki Ryoho Kyogi, which is what we in the West refer to as the Reiki principles, and the Kokai Denju Setsumei, a questions and answer session about Reiki with the answers coming from Usui sensei and the questions coming from his students in the Usui Reiki Ryoho Gakkai. Also included is the original Japanese text from these two sections. The titles are translated into both Rōmaji (which gives the Japanese pronunciation in Roman characters) and English. The remaining two sections of the workbook, Ryoho Shishin, guidelines for treatment, and Meiji Tenno Gyosei, the Emperor Meiji's poems, may be included in a future issue of the magazine.

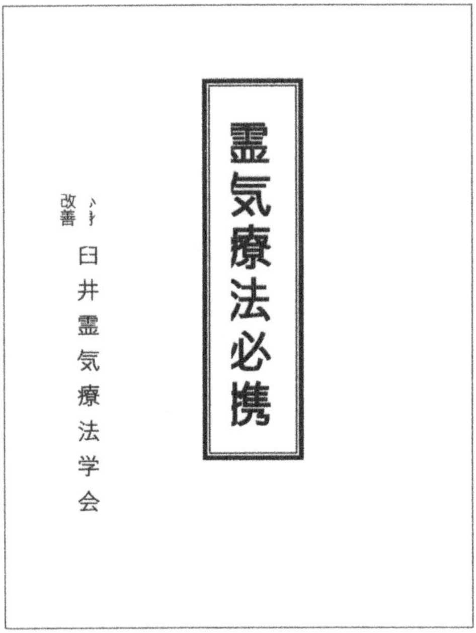
霊気療法必携
心身改善 臼井霊気療法学会

霊気療法必携

Reiki Ryoho Hikkei
Reiki Healing Art Handbook

心身改善 臼 井 霊 気 療 法 学 会

Shinshin kaizen
USUI REIKI RYOHO GAKKAI
Mind/body improvement
USUI REIKI RYOHO GAKKAI

ハト改善
臼井霊気療法教義
招福の秘法
萬病の霊薬
今日丈けは怒るな
心配すな感謝して

目次
一、臼井霊気療法教義
二、公開伝授説明
三、療法指針
四、明治天皇御製

Contents

1. Usui Reiki Ryoho Kyogi (Usui Reiki Healing Art Principles)
2. Kokai Denju Setsumei (An Explanation of Open Teaching)
3. Ryoho Shishin (Guidelines for treatment)
4. Meiji Tenno Gyosei (The Emperor Meiji's poems)

Mind/body improvement
USUI REIKI RYOHO KYOGI
(PRINCIPLES)
Secret method to invite happiness
Miraculous medicine to cure all diseases
Today Only, Do Not Anger
Do Not Worry, Be grateful
Work diligently, Be kind to others.
Mornings and evenings
With Gassho hands
Bearing these words in mind
Chant them

公 開 伝 授 説 明

EXPLANATION OF OPEN TEACHING

From olden days till now, when one created or discovered an original and mystic teaching, he tended only to teach it to his own children, making the teaching a privilege of the family and claiming that the contents of the teaching should be kept confidential within the family, so as to scheme for financial security of one's posterity. That can be said to be an outdated custom of the last century. It is absolutely not acceptable to privately monopolize a teaching in modern times when co-existence and co-prosperity of humanity underlie happiness and also when social development is desired.

公開伝授説明

肇祖 臼井甕男

古来能く独自の秘法を創見するや、已か子孫にのみ教えて家伝と為し之に依って後生一門の生活安定を計り、秘法内容の門外不出を唱うるが如きは実に前世紀の遺習と申すもので、苟も現在の如く人類の共存共栄を以て幸福の基調となし、併せて社会の進歩を要望す

2

開放し、何人をも共に天恵に欲せしめ、以て霊肉一如を期し、人世天与の福祉を得しめんとするものであります。元より我が霊気療法は宇宙間の霊能に基づ霊気の独創療法でありますから、此れに依って先ず人間自體を壮健にし、思想の穏健と人生の愉悦を増進するの

3

My Usui Reiki Ryoho (healing art) is original, never before explored, and incomparable in the world. Therefore, it is to be made available for the good of humankind, so that anyone may be blessed with this heavenly gift, that the soul and body may be as one, and heaven-sent well-being may be realized in one's life. Because my Reiki Ryoho is a unique and original art of healing based on the healing power of the universe, a person first becomes healthy and then soundness of thought and the joys of life are enhanced.

The reason I venture to teach openly, at a time like today when improvement and reconstruction of our lives within and without is essential, is to save all fellow countrymen from troubled minds and from sickness and diseases.

Q.) What is Usui Reiki Ryoho?

A.) Receiving with profound awe and reverence the teachings of the Emperor Meiji, achieving our Principles, and intending to train and develop the mind and body. First, the mind should be healed, and secondly the physical body be made healthy so as to walk on the right path of humanity. If the mind is healthy, conforming to a path of integrity, then the body becomes sturdy of its own accord.

The mission of Usui Reiki Ryoho is to enhance mutual well-being for oneself and others, on the one hand, by fulfilling a peaceful and joyful life mentally and physically and, on the other, by healing the sick.

Q.) Is Usui Reiki Ryoho the same as hypnotism, the art of mental healing with Ki-ai, faith healing, and the like, just with a different name?
A.) No, it is not the same as these other techniques. It is the art of healing the mind and body, which I have realized as a mystic after many years of hard and difficult training.

Q.) Then, is it the art of a spiritual healing?
A.) Yes, it can be called the art of a spiritual healing, however, it can also be called the art of a physical healing. The reason for it is that any part of the physical body of a practitioner may radiate the energy and light, particularly from the eyes, mouth, and hands. Therefore, by means of gazing at for a few minutes, or blowing on, or stroking the affected part, toothache, colic, stomachache, neuralgia, breast tumor, bruises, cuts, burns, and other swellings and pains can quickly be relieved and be gone. However, chronic diseases are not easy to cure. Several treatments are required; yet even a chronic disease becomes better with one treatment.

There is fact beyond fiction. I wonder how modern medicine can explain this kind of phenomena. If you actually see the fact, you will be sure to acknowledge it. Even those who play around with sophistry cannot ignore the fact.

Q.) Does one need to believe in Usui Reiki Ryoho so that an illness can be cured?
A.) No, unlike psychological therapy, hypnotism, and other mental healing modalities, no consent nor esteem is required, for not a single suggestion is given. Moreover, it matters little whether you may doubt, avoid, and deny that. For instance, there is a positive effect on those who lack consciousness, such as infants and/or seriously ill patients. Barely one out of ten people trust and esteem my art of healing before they experience it the first time. Most people come to trust suddenly after having received treatment once and acknowledged its effect.

Q.) Can any disease be cured by Usui Reiki Ryoho?
A.) Any disease, mental or organic, can be cured.

Q.) Does Usui Reiki Ryoho cure diseases only?

A.) No, not only cure diseases of a physical body but also mental illnesses i.e., anguish, weakness, cowardice, vacillation, nervousness, and other bad habits can be cured. And emphasis is placed on healing others with god-like or Buddha-like mind, and happiness can be mutually shared with other people.

Q.) Why and how does Usui Reiki Ryoho work?
A.) I have not been taught this art of healing by anyone under the heavens, nor have I studied in order to obtain this mysterious ability to heal. I accidentally realized that I was given this mysterious healing ability when I felt the great power and was inspired by the mystery during a period of fasting. Therefore, even as the founder, I find it difficult to give a sure explanation. Scientists and intellectuals have been eagerly researching and consider it difficult to confirm with modern science, yet the time will surely come when science can prove it.

Q.) Does Usui Reiki Ryoho use medicine and is there any harmful effect?
A.) Medicine and instruments are never employed. Diseases can be cured just by gazing, blowing, stroking, pressing, and patting.

Q.) Does Usui Reiki Ryoho require medical knowledge?
A.) My Ryoho (healing art) is not based on medicine, for it is a wondrous energy work that rises above modern science. The purpose of curing can be fulfilled just by gazing, or blowing, or pressing, or stroking the affected part, for instance, the head, if there's a brain trouble, or the stomach, if there's a stomach trouble, or the eyes, if there's an eye trouble, etc. Thus, the diseases can be cured in a short time without taking bitter medicines or receiving moxibustion. That is the reason my Reiho (wondrous energy work) is unique and original.

Q.) What is the perspective of well-known medical professionals of today?
A.) The perspective of well-informed and well-known medical people is truly moderate and reasonable. Famous European medical professionals severely criticize medicine. Apart from that, Dr. Nagai Hisomu of Imperial Medical College says that we, medical professionals, know how to diagnose the diseases, write them down and understand them, but we do not know how to cure them. Dr. Kondo says that it is very delusive to say medicine has greatly advanced. A big fault in modern medicine is that function of the mind has been disregarded. Dr. Hara Sakae says it is an extreme indignity that our modern hygienic medicine has ignored the intelligence of human beings and has come to treat them in the same

way as other animals. I do believe that there will be a great revolution in the field of medical treatment in the near future. Dr. Rokuro Kuga says it is true that psychotherapy and other therapies are bringing about a far better result, by applying an appropriate treatment according to a disease and patient's personality, than a practice of medical professionals.

It is narrow-minded of medical professionals to blindly resist and boycott non-medical people and psychotherapists. (From Japan Medical News) These remarks are evident, for it is a fact that medical doctors, medical practitioners, and pharmacists are in fact becoming students and acknowledging the efficacy of Reiki Ryoho.

Q.) What is the Government's view?
A.) At the Budget sub-committee of the Imperial Diet's House of Representatives held on February 6th in the year of Taisho (1922), Dr. Matsushita Teiji, a Diet member, inquired about the Government's view regarding non-medical professionals treating many patients in the name of psychotherapy or mental therapy. Mr. Ushio, a Government committeeman, responded, "Until 10 years ago hypnotism was considered to be the art done by Tengu (an imaginary long-nosed creature in the mountains). Today, however, after the accumulation of studies, it is accepted and applied to treating patients with mental problems. It is difficult to solve all human issues through medicine. Medical practitioners apply this or that treatment to this or that disease according to medical expertise. However, treatments by means of an electric device or by means of touching are not considered a medical practice." Therefore my Usui Reiki Ryoho does not violate either the medical law or the acupuncture/moxibustion regulations.

Q.) I don't think just anyone can learn and practice this because such an ability to heal is a godsend bestowed upon a special person. What do you say?
A.) Not at all, each and every being has an innate ability to heal as a gift from gods. As with grass, trees, birds, fish, and insects, humans particularly, as the lords of all creation, develop the healing ability to a greater degree. Usui Reiki Ryoho has appeared in the world as the embodiment of that gift.

Q.) Then, can anyone receive Usui Reiki Ryoho teaching?
A.) Of course, anyone at least with common sense – man or woman, young or old, educated or uneducated – can surely acquire the ability to cure their own disease, as well as that of others, in a short period of time. So far I have taught over a thousand people, and not a single person has failed. All of those with only

Shoden (first level) have acquired the ability to cure diseases successfully. Come to think of it, it seems unbelievable to become able, in a short period time, to gain the ability to heal diseases, which is the most difficult task for us as humans. But I find it to be a very natural thing. It is a particular feature of my Reiho that the most difficult task can be easily done.

Q.) So let's say then that we can cure the disease of others, but can we cure our own disease?
A.) How can we cure others if we are unable to cure ourselves?

Q.) What should one do to advance to Okuden (the second level)?
A.) In the Okuden teachings there is Hatsurei Ho, Uchite Chiryo Ho, Nadete Chiryo Ho, Oshite Chiryo Ho, Enkaku Chiryo Ho, Seiheki Chiryo Ho, and others. First of all, one should receive Shoden, and then Okuden shall be taught to those with excellence in practice, high morals, integrity, and earnestness about the path.

Q.) Is there anything above and beyond Okuden in Reiki Ryoho?
A.) There is Shinpiden (mystery teaching).

Reiki Before Usui

BY WILLIAM LEE RAND

This article first appeared in the December, 2013 edition of the Reiki Online Newsletter. *It is part of a series of articles based on the historical research methods described in the article, "An Evidence Based History of Reiki," which appeared in the October 2013 edition of the* Reiki Online Newsletter *and in the Fall 2013 issue of* Reiki News Magazine. *The purpose of these articles is to dispel the myths about the history and practice of Reiki that first appeared in Western Reiki and have developed since then. It is important that an understanding of Reiki be based on verified facts so that its true nature will be understood, appreciated and practiced.*

MANY IN THE REIKI COMMUNITY think that Reiki is something that Usui Sensei developed and that the word should only be applied to his system of healing. But even a cursory examination of the historical evidence reveals that the word Reiki had been in the Japanese lexicon long before Usui Sensei used it. Furthermore, there were other healing systems in existence before Usui Reiki was developed that used the name Reiki and/or used Reiki energy. Clearly, Reiki is a name that isn't exclusive to Usui Reiki but can be applied to any style of healing that uses Reiki energy.

It is an unfortunate legacy of the Western style of Reiki that there were many unverified ideas that were included in its teaching that have subsequently been revealed to be false. One example is the history of Usui Reiki that was originally told in the West, which has been shown through evidence based research to contain many exaggerations and false ideas.

Those who love Reiki and have respect for Usui Sensei and his method of healing will want to know and perpetuate the facts based on historical evidence rather than continue to hold onto beliefs that were previously thought to be true. In order to do this, it's necessary to have humility and discipline and the level of critical thinking required to let go of one's cherished beliefs in order to accept the more accurate information that has been verified. After all, if a Reiki teacher wants to provide a meaningful service to her students, it's important to make use of verified facts. Fortunately, there are many who acknowledge the value of this level of thinking and are applying it to the practice and teaching of Reiki. In this way, greater harmony is coming to the Reiki community as each teacher and school bases its understanding of Reiki on ideas that anyone can verify. This level of thinking also helps bring Reiki into alignment with professional standards thus making it more acceptable by mainstream society including the medical and scientific communities.

History of the Japanese Language

The Japanese did not have a written language until the seventh century AD when writing became widespread.[1] The system of writing that was developed was based on Chinese ideograms. This system of Chinese characters were first developed around 1200 BC and was standardized during the Han Dynasty (206 BC – 220 AD) resulting in hanzi or kanji as they are called in Japanese. Because of this, many Japanese and Chinese concepts are written using the same characters, making it possible for the Japanese to have an understanding of Chinese writing and vice versa. The hanzi ideograms for rei and ki were introduced to Japan at this time. In Chinese these ideograms are pronounced ling and qi respectively and have similar meanings as they do in Japanese. This indicates that the root concept for Reiki is several thousand years old.[2]

It is not known exactly when Rei and Ki were joined together to form a word; further research is necessary to determine the date and how it was used. But current understanding is that it was sometime after the written Japanese language developed and before it was used by Usui Sensei.

The following is a definition for each of the Reiki kanji provided by Hiroshi Doi, Japanese Gendai Reiki Ho founder and member of the Usui Reiki Ryoho Gakkai:

The Kanji of 靈 rei has 3 parts; one 雨, three 口 and one 巫.

1. 雨 ame (rain), is a blessing from the Great Universe. It showers down from the sky above, allows living things to grow on the ground, and heals and cleanses everything.
2. Three squares (originally circles) mean the three elements of a human being; body, mind and soul.
3. 巫 means 巫女 (miko) medium who channels God's will and her mission is to connect heaven and earth. That is to say, the original meaning of 靈 is the unity of the Great Universe with a human being.

[1] Bjarke Frellesvig, *History of the Japanese Language* (Cambridge, UK: Cambridge University Press, 2010) p. 12.

[2] Noriko Kurosawa Williams, *The Key to Kanji, A Visual History of 1100 Characters* (Boston, MA: Cheng & Tsui Company, Inc, 2010) 1; P. G. O'Neill, *Essential Kanji* (New York: Weatherhill, Inc, 1973) p. 44, 189.

The Kanji of 氣 ki is divided into 2 parts.

1. 气, which is said to be formed from the shape of steam or a cloud.
2. The other part, 米, read kome, meaning a staple food like rice.

氣 represents the energy of boiling steam that pushes up the heavy lid of a pot of cooking rice.

The ancient Chinese recognized human breathing, wind (breathing of nature), fog, cloud and steam as 氣. They thought that 1) 氣 is an ever-changing, gaseous material that is ubiquitous and flows everywhere in the universe including in the human body. 2) 氣 is the primal essence of everything in the universe and it is the source of life force and energies that create our physical and mental functions.

Therefore 靈氣 Reiki is the energy of life that is being guided by the Great Universe (the Universal Being of Wisdom and Love) and can be channeled by those who have received this special ability.

Mataji Kawakami

In an email I received September 29, 2013, Doi Sensei said he had been an honorary advisor for the Global Holistic Healing Association in Japan, an organization that practiced Usui Reiki. Katsuyuki Takashahi was a supporting member who wrote a newsletter called *Holistic Healing*. In the February 2003 issue of the newsletter he included a note about Mataji Kawakami, who was a Ryojutsu-ka (therapist) and president of Trinity Research. Kawakami founded a healing practice he called 霊気療法 Reiki Ryoho in 1914. He had the term Reiki Ryoho recognized by the medical and educational experts of the time and wrote a book titled, *Reiki Ryoho to Sono Koka*, 霊気療法とその効果, *Reiki Healing and its Effects*, which was published in 1919.

According to Doi Sensei and Toshitaka Mochizuki, another esteemed Japanese Reiki sensei and author, there were several other Reiki healing methods being practiced in Japan prior to Usui Reiki Ryoho. These include: 霊感透熱療法 Reikan Tonetsu Ryoho created by Reikaku Ishinuki, 洗心流霊気療法 Senshin-ryu Reiki Ryoho created by Kogetsu Matsubara and 生道霊掌術 Seido Reisho-jutsu created by Reisen Oyama.[3]

[3] Email communication received November 10, 2013 from Doi Sensei through his interpreter, Fumi Koji; Toshitaka Mochitzuki, *Iyashi No Te* (Healing Hands), (Tokyo, Japan: Tama Shuppan, 1995).

It is also important to note that Usui Sensei didn't call his system of healing Reiki; he called it Shin-shin Kai-Zen Usui Reiki Ryoho (The Usui Reiki Treatment Method for Improvement of Body and Mind) or in the shorter version, Usui Reiki Ryoho. This indicates that Usui Sensei understood that what he developed was his style of Reiki healing, not the only style.

So from this information we can see that Reiki isn't a name that applies only to the system of healing Usui Sensei developed, but can be used by any system of healing that uses Reiki energy.

Reiki Energy Defined

So what is Reiki energy and how can we recognize it? In The *Spirit of Reiki*, a book published in 2001 that I wrote along with Arjava Petter and Walter Lubeck, there is a definition of Reiki on page 22. It explains that Reiki is any healing energy that fulfills the following four criteria:

1. The ability to perform Reiki comes from having received an attunement, rather than developing the ability over time through the use of meditation or other exercises.
2. All Reiki techniques are part of a lineage, meaning the technique has been passed from teacher to student through an attunement process, starting with [the founder of the technique].
3. Reiki does not require that one guide the energy with the mind, as it is guided by the higher power that knows what vibration or combination of vibrations [are needed by the client].
4. Reiki can do no harm.[4]

I hope this gives you a better understanding and appreciation for Reiki. I encourage you to use Reiki more frequently to bring happiness and healing to yourself and to those who come to you for help. May you always be blessed by the love and wisdom of the Universe.

[4] Walter Lubeck, Frank Arjava Petter, and William Rand, *The Spirit of Reiki* (Twin Lakes, WI: Lotus Press, 2001) p. 22.

The Story of Dr. Chujiro Hayashi

BY MARIANNE STREICH

WE IN THE WEST KNOW Reiki today because Dr. Chujiro Hayashi agreed to teach it to an American woman of Japanese descent. Hawayo Takata's teachings caused Reiki to spread around the world—and to return to Japan. As interest in Reiki has rekindled in its land of origin, more information has become available regarding Hayashi's teachings and practice.

We know little about Hayashi's personal life beyond basic facts. He was born September 15, 1880. He graduated from the Japan Naval Academy in 1902 as a medical doctor. He married, and he and his wife Chie had two children. He served in the Russo-Japanese War from 1902-1906, achieved the rank of captain, and in 1918 was appointed Director of Ominato Port Defense Station on the Shimokita Peninsula in the North of Japan.

Rear Admiral Kan'ichi Taketomi was Chief of Staff at the station at the time. Taketomi later become the third chairman of the *Usui Reiki Ryoho Gakkai*. It is likely that Hayashi learned about Reiki from him or from other naval officers, as several had trained with Usui. Hayashi became *Shihan* (teacher) in 1925 at age 46, after his retirement from the navy.[1] He may have been the last person to receive *Shihan* from Usui Sensei, since Usui died in 1926.

Usui asked Hayashi to establish a Reiki clinic to further the work of the *Gakkai*, which Hayashi did, opening a clinic in Shinano-machi, Tokyo[2] and sub-

[1] Hiroshi Doi. *Modern Reiki Method for Healing* (B.C., Canada: Fraser Journal Publishing, 2000), p. 49.

[2] Ibid.

sequently establishing branches in other cities. After Usui's death Hayashi left the *Gakkai* and formed the *Hayashi Reiki Kenkyukai* (institute). Although he developed his own style, Hayashi continued to honor Usui's lineage. Certificates were issued under the name of *Hayashi Reiki Kenkyukai*, but they carry the name *Shinshin Kaizen Usui Reiki Ryoho*, or Mind/Body Improvement Usui Reiki Ryoho, to signify that *Usui Reiki Ryoho* was instructed.[3]

A 1928 article published in a widely circulated Japanese magazine characterized Hayashi as "...a diligent warm-hearted naval captain who looks as if he was born to be a Reiki practitioner...."[4] The author, Mr. Shou Matsui, an actor and playwright who had introduced a number of his fellow actors to Reiki, lamented the fact that Usui had not wished to publicize Reiki and that Hayashi was also unwilling to make his work known. Mr. Matsui was so convinced of its effectiveness he wanted everyone to know about Reiki.

In 1937 Hayashi travelled to Hawaii with his daughter and stayed for several months, hosted by Takata. He gave free lectures about Reiki with Takata demonstrating. Before he left Hawaii in February of 1938, he awarded her a *Shihan* certificate.[5] After he returned home, the Japanese naval authority asked him to give information about Hawaii, and when he failed to cooperate, he was accused of being a spy. Finding himself in an untenable position, he chose to end his life honorably through the ritual of *seppuku (suicide through disembowelment)*. He died on May 11, 1940.[6]

Hayashi's wife Chie took over the clinic after his death. She travelled to the various branches and taught Reiki as he had. Neither of their two children followed in their parents' footsteps, and the Hayashi institute died out after Chie stopped teaching. In 1952 Takata attended one of the yearly memorial services held to honor Hayashi. It is said that during that visit, Chie Hayashi suggested that Takata return to Japan and take over the *Hayashi Reiki Kenkyu-kai*, but Takata declined.[7]

[3] William Lee Rand, "An Interview with Hiroshi Doi," *Reiki News Magazine* (Fall 2003), p. 13.

[4] Frank Arjava Petter, Tado Yamaguchi, and Chujiro Hayashi. *The Hayashi Reiki Manual, Traditional Japanese Healing Techniques from the Founder of the Western Reiki System* (Wisconsin: Lotus Press, 2003), p. 30.

[5] Helen Joyce Haberly. *Reiki: Hawayo Takata's Story* (Maryland: Archedigm Publications, 2000 Memorial Edition), p. 33.

[6] Tadao Yamaguchi, *Light on the Origins of Reiki, A Handbook for Practicing the Original Reiki of Usui and Hayashi.* (Wisconsin: Lotus Press, 2007), p. 69.

[7] Petter, p. 27.

Differences in Usui and Hayashi's styles

In addition to asking Hayashi to open a Reiki clinic, Usui also asked him to further develop Reiki based on his medical knowledge. During an interview published in the Fall 2003 issue of *Reiki News Magazine*,[8] Hiroshi Doi described the differences between the Hayashi style and that of the Usui style practiced by the Gakkai. At the *Gakkai*, recipients were to sit when receiving treatment, unless they were seriously ill. Hayashi changed this to have the recipient lie on a table. Usui's treatments were one-on-one; Hayashi had two or more practitioners treat each recipient. Hayashi developed an original hands-on system, and a new handbook was issued, *Reiki Ryoho Shinshin*, or "Guidelines for Reiki Healing Method." He also developed a new system of conferring and passing on Reiki *Ryoho* and established a monthly, five-day workshop during which *Okuden* was given. The *Gakkai* placed emphasis on the navel and the Tanden as important energy centers, while Hayashi focused more on the meridian lines of acupuncture and the chakras. Usui referenced various vertebrae in relation to hand positions; Hayashi's reference was to the organs.

Hayashi taught monthly classes in Tokyo and Osaka. He taught twice each year in Ishikawa at the Daishoji branch. It is believed there were other branches as well, as Hayashi taught all over Japan.[9] The attunement was given first, followed by a lecture explaining the nature of Reiki. Prior to an attunement, Hayashi had students sit in front of a scroll that he had drawn depicting *Gokai* (the Five Ideals or Principles) and follow him in reciting the Principles. He instructed his teachers to do so as well, because the scroll "has great energy which cleanses the venue."[10] Reciting *Gokai* purified the venue and readied it for *Reiju* (attunement). He also recited, and at times had students recite, *Gyosei* (poems written by the Meiji Emperor) before giving *Reiju*.[11] Each recipient was attuned by each *Shihan* present, one after the other. Emphasis was placed on receiving regular attunements and students attended monthly meetings during which they received *Reiju-kai*, or attunement sessions.[12] Monthly sessions were also held at the branch in Ishikawa so that participants could receive *Reiju* from local *Shihans*, even though Hayashi was not present.[13]

[8] Rand, p. 13–14.

[9] Ibid., p. 16–17.

[10] Yamaguchi, p. 144.

[11] Ibid., p. 83.

[12] Ibid., p. 28.

[13] Ibid., p. 29.

This article relies heavily on information made available by Tadao Yamaguchi through his book, *Light on the Origins of Reiki* and through Frank Arjava Petter's book, *The Hayashi Reiki Manual*. Yamaguchi's mother, Chiyoko Yamaguchi, received her first attunement from Hayashi in 1938 when she was 17 years old.[14] She received subsequent training from her uncle, Mr. Wasaburo Sugano, and with Hayashi's approval, became *Shihan* in the autumn of 1939, in less time than was typical.[15] She practiced Reiki quietly in Japan for 65 years, until her passing in 2003. Her perspective is invaluable for understanding how Hayashi taught and practiced Reiki. Her recounting of the first attunement she received from Hayashi evokes a powerful sense of what it must have been like to be present during *Reiju-kai* with him.

Chiyoko Yamaguchi's First Attunement

Chiyoko's older sister and other family members practiced Reiki, and she eagerly awaited the day when she would be attuned as well. Her uncle required her to wait until she graduated from high school. When the day finally arrived, she dressed in a new kimono given to her by her uncle for the occasion and went with her sister Katsue to the seminar, which began at 10 AM. The youngest person present by some years, she felt slightly intimidated by the formal atmosphere and impressively attired *Shihans*.

Coordinators of the event greeted participants and explained how they were to receive *Reiju*. They were instructed to sit in the *seiza* posture (formal Japanese sitting posture with legs folded beneath the body so that one is sitting on one's heels) with their eyes closed, sitting straight and taking care not to put pressure on the Tanden (a spot just below the navel). It was explained that those giving the attunements would touch the participant to indicate they should place their hands in *Gassho* as the attunement began. Once their hands were in *Gassho*, the *Shihan* would place one hand on the head and give the attunement. They were told a second attunement would be given with the *Shihan's* hands around the *Gassho* hands of the participant. They were not to stand up or to talk, but wait quietly until all had been attuned.

Once they had been briefed, Hayashi Sensei entered the room dressed in *Haoari* and *Hakama* (traditional formal Japanese suit-type kimono). Chiryo described him as a tall, dignified man with impressive bearing who seemed to have a light shining all around him. With Hayashi leading, participants recit-

[14] Petter, p. 16.

[15] Ibid., p. 26.

ed the *Gokai* (The Five Reiki Ideals or Principles). He began with kyo dake wa (just for today) and participants repeated this and the remaining lines in unison three times:

kyo dake wa (just for today)
ikaru-na (do not get angry)
shinpaisuna (do not worry)
kansha shite (be thankful)
gyo hageme (work hard)
hito-ni shinsetsu-ni (be kind to others)[16]

Next, the light was turned off and the shutters closed so that the room was very dark. Hayashi Sensei performed the *Reiju*, followed by other *Shihans*. Each *Reiju* lasted about five minutes. Hayashi chanted *Gyosei* of the Meiji Emperor throughout the attunement.[17]

After the attunement students performed *Reiki Mawashi* (Reiki circulating practice) by forming a circle and placing their hands on the back of the person in front of them, remaining in that position for 10-20 minutes. Sometimes Hayashi joined in the circle; at other times, he sat in the center, directing participants. This was followed by a lecture and then, in the afternoon, practical application.[18]

After attunements had been given, Hayashi explained the theory behind Reiki.[19] He told his students, "Reiki cures problems from the bottom up."[20] Hayashi talked about diseases of the day and discussed the body's natural healing process and how Reiki activates it. He used the metaphor of a muddy stream, telling students that Reiki stirs up stagnant energy, just as sediment will surface when a stream is disturbed. As surface sediment is removed, the stream will appear to be clearer, although some sediment will sink to the bottom again. Continuing the process of bringing sediment to the surface and removing it will ulti-

[16] The Gokai or Five Reiki Ideals may be heard in Japanese at www.reiki.org and are available on CD from Inner Worlds Music, *Merlin's Magic, Reiki Space of Peace and Love* (track #4).

[17] Gyosei are waka—classical Japanese verse of five lines containing 5-7-5-7-7 syllables. When written by an emperor they are known as Gyosei.

[18] Yamaguchi, p. 30–36; Petter, p. 18–25.

[19] Petter, p. 18–20.

[20] Yamaguchi, p. 133.

mately result in a clear stream. Just as a disturbed stream will appear muddy, disturbing stagnant energy can result in a healing reaction or in symptoms temporarily getting worse, but as the stagnant energy continues to be removed, the body becomes clear, just as the stream becomes clear if the muddy sediment is removed. He described healing as the process of making the finest paper, in which each sheet is peeled off until the healthy being is revealed.[21] He showed an anatomical chart and discussed the function of each organ and the application of Reiki depending on the symptoms presented.[22]

In the afternoon, students gave and received treatments and also treated people from the neighborhood who were in poor health.

Handbooks

The Hayashi Reiki *Kenkyukai* [Hayashi Reiki Institute] published a treatment manual, *Ryoho Shishin*, which gave guidelines for treatment according to symptoms and diseases.[23] Usui's manual placed emphasis on hand positions as they relate to the spine,[24] while Hayashi's manual relates hand positions to the various organs. For instance, under "Flu" Hayashi's handbook gives the following listing: 1. Nose, 2. Throat, 3. Trachea, 4. Bronchus, 5. Lungs, 6. Liver, 7. Pancreas, 8. Stomach, 9. Intestines, 10. Kidneys, 11. Head, 12. *Kekko* Massage. Although the areas for treatment are given, this does not indicate that a certain order of hand positions should be followed. Unlike the teaching of Western Reiki, Hayashi did not teach a progressive sequence for hand positions. [25]

According to Yamaguchi, entries in the manual were intended to give direction when the practitioner was unable to discover *Byosen*. The practitioner was to lay hands on the suggested areas until the *Byosen* was located. Takata told Fran Brown that each of Hayashi's students was given "...a list of complaints and places to look for the cause."[26] John Gray, one of Takata's Masters, was given Takata's copy of this 40-page handbook. Alongside the normal *kanji*, were written simple Japanese characters that would have been used for

[21] Ibid., p. 70, 72.

[22] Ibid., p. 75.

[23] A translation of this manual can be found in *Reiki, The Healing Touch* by William Lee Rand.

[24] See Frank Arjava Petter, *The Original Reiki Handbook of Dr. Mikao Usui* (Wisconsin: Lotus Press, 1999).

[25] Yamaguchi, p. 124.

[26] Fran Brown. *Living Reiki, Takata's Teachings* (California: LifeRhythm, 1992), p. 30.

children or those not fluent in Japanese. It is likely that this was done because Takata's ability to read Japanese was not as acute as her ability to speak it.[27]

Hayashi also gave his students a booklet of 100 of the 125 poems Usui had selected from the thousands written by the Meiji Emperor. They contained sayings for "improvement of body and mind," such as, "Things are apt to go in an unexpected way. What you have to mind is your own mind itself."[28] These *Gyosei* were considered as important to the practice of Reiki as the *Gokai* or Five Ideals. Yamaguchi provides translations of a few of them in his book.[29]

Degrees and classes

Although degrees and classes differ somewhat from those given in Western Reiki, they do correspond in a general way as listed below:

Shoden (first term)—Western Level I
Okuden (second term)—Western Level II
Shinpiden (mystery teaching)—Western Master

Shoden consisted of four levels, which were called the 6th degree (lowest), 5th, 4th, and 3rd. Each level consisted of a three-hour seminar followed by a practical session of giving treatments.[30] According to Tadao Yamaguchi, during *Shoden* participants learned the first symbol and the *Ketsueki Kokan (Kekko)* technique, which translates as "blood exchange" method but is a means of improving circulation through massage.[31] They practiced Reiki *Mawashi* and Reiki *Okuri* (sending Reiki with palms facing each other but not touching). They also learned *Hatsurei-ho*, or the method for radiating Reiki. This was a five-day individual exercise regime that takes 30-40 minutes to perform and is a means of increasing the flow of Reiki. They also spent time each day of the class with hands-on practice.

[27] John Harvey Gray and Lourdes Gray with Steven McFadden and Elisabeth Clark, *Hand to Hand, the Longest-Practicing Reiki Master Tells His Story* (Gray, 2002), p. 183.

[28] Yamaguchi, p. 83.

[29] Ibid., p. 83–88.

[30] Petter, p. 15.

[31] See Petter, p. 51–61, for an illustrated, detailed explanation of the steps in Kekko. Yamaguchi describes the process on pages 128–130 in his book.

Takata told Fran Brown that *Shoden* was completed in four days. The first day the focus was on the basic positions above the neck and the diseases they treated. During day two, treatment of the front of the body was discussed, the back positions on day three, and acute cases and accidents on day four.[32]

Okuden was divided into two sessions, *Okunden-Zenki* and *Okuden*-Koki. "Students were allowed to participate in the *Okuden* training course only after a lot of practice, which would enable them to feel *Byosen* (problematic areas)..."[33] This typically took about three months, but could take up to six months or a year. However, Hayashi Sensei did give an intensive five-day course of both *Shoden* and *Okuden* coupled with longer hours each day when he taught outside Toyko and Osaka."[34] During the *Okuden* class they received the Mental/Emotional symbol and learned how to use it for treatment of psychological issues and trauma. They also learned to send distant treatment and received the Distant Healing *Jumon* (mantra). According to Petter, students learned *Ketsueki Kokan* at the *Okuden* level.[35]

Shinpiden consisted of two levels, *Shihan-Kaku* or assistant teacher, permitted to teach the *Shoden* course, and *Shihan* or teacher, permitted to teach both *Shoden* and *Okuden*. "The *Shihan* degrees were not given in a seminar the way they are today. When a person was [deemed] ready [by Hayashi], he or she was able to learn to give *Reiju* privately."[36] Hayashi determined when a practitioner who had completed *Okuden* had practiced sufficiently and was qualified to receive *Shihan*; moving to this level was not by choice of the practitioner. Hayashi gave some *Shihans* permission to teach teachers.[37] The symbols and methods of attunement were not written down but were passed as an oral tradition by both Usui and Hayashi.[38]

[32] Brown, p. 29.

[33] Yamaguchi, p. 28.

[34] Ibid., p. 28.

[35] Petter, p. 51.

[36] Yamaguchi, p. 36. It is my sense that Takata probably conferred the Master degree in this way. There is little information regarding this, but to my knowledge, only one of her Masters, Fran Brown, speaks of having formal training for the Master level. In her book *Living Reiki, Takata's Teachings*, Brown recounts having spent a week snow-bound with Takata and receiving Master training during that time; however, she does not mention the number of hours or a curriculum for the training.

[37] Yamaguchi, p. 140.

[38] Ibid., p. 15.

Symbols

According to Yamaguchi,[39] students were not attuned to the symbols; the symbols were simply introduced. He makes a distinction between symbols (*Shirushi*) and mantras (*Jumon*). The Power symbol and Mental/Emotional symbols are symbols; what we consider the Distant Healing symbol is a *Jumon* or mantra. This explains why it is comprised of *kanji* that can be found in any Japanese dictionary. One does not say the name of a symbol when it is drawn, as we do in the West; however, one simultaneously draws and repeats a *Jumon*.[40] The power of a *Jumon* is in saying it aloud.[41]

Yamaguchi says of the Power symbol: "... [it] signifies the highest place, that which humans cannot reach which is the source of Reiki. Usui Sensei took it from a Shinto concept and it is used to focus energy to tackle *Byosen*."[42] Hayashi advised his students not to overuse it. The Mental/Emotional symbol is based on a Sanskrit letter and is used specifically for psychological treatment. According to Doi, Usui did not teach or use a Master symbol nor was it used in attunements and the *Gakkai* do not use this symbol. However, Takata did have a Master symbol and Rand's thinking is that since Mrs. Yamaguchi learned Reiki from Hayashi and didn't have this symbol, even though she was taught how to give attunements 2 years after Takata learned, it isn't likely that Hayashi used this symbol either. Since Takata is the one who created a different attunement for each level and used attunements to empower the symbols, it is likely that she is the one who added the Master symbol, perhaps as a way to add value to the Master level and make it a requirement to give attunements so only those who paid her high fee and received the Master symbol and its attunement would be able to teach.[43]

Hayashi's Clinic

Hayashi's clinic in central Tokyo had eight tables. Two practitioners typically worked with each client, although at times there was an additional practitioner. Tables were rattan beds 30-40 cm (11.81–15.75 inches) high. Futons were used if additional beds were needed. Practitioners sat on the floor.[44]

[39] Ibid., p. 140–147.

[40] Ibid., p. 141.

[41] Ibid., p. 151.

[42] Ibid., p. 147.

[43] Telephone conversation with William Rand, August 8, 2009.

[44] Ibid., p. 33.

One practitioner began with the head while the second treated the problem area. If there were a third practitioner, he or she would treat the feet. The soles of the feet were considered next in importance to the head. Practitioners located *Byosen* and gave Reiki intensely at that location until the *Byosen* eased. Hayashi taught that they should always treat the head and always end with *Kekko* massage. The sequence for treating the head was forehead, back of head, temples, and crown.[45]

Takata reported that during the year she lived with the Hayashi family and received training, she gave treatments along with other practitioners from 7 AM until noon. One practitioner worked on the client's head, the other on the stomach area, then both worked on the back. Practitioners received a one hour lunch break and then in the afternoon made house calls, giving treatments that typically lasted from one to one and one-half hours. They returned home by 7 PM.[46]

Treatment Methods

The purpose of Reiki in Usui and Hayashi's day was to heal physical illness.[47] All diseases were treated and the handbooks issued by the *Gakkai* and the *Kenkyu-kai* focused on how to treat specific illnesses. *Byosen* and *Ketsueki Kokan Ho (Kekko)* massage were considered essential techniques for any treatment.

Although some Western practitioners use *Byosen* scanning, it was not a technique specifically taught by Takata. She may have made reference to it when she said, "Reiki will guide you. Let your Reiki hands find it. They will know what to do."[48] *Ketsueki Kokan Ho* is not widely practiced in the West, partly because Takata did not teach it, but perhaps also because of practitioners' concerns that one might need a massage license to use the technique.

Several other techniques were used by Usui and Hayashi that were not taught by Takata. Yamaguchi quotes the *Reiki Ryoho no Shiori* (Reiki Treatment Guidelines) issued by the *Gakkai*: "Treatment is carried out by gazing at affected areas, blowing onto them, patting, rubbing or laying hands on them."[49] For instance, to treat burns, one first employed *Gyo-shi* (eye Reiki) by gazing at the affected area, followed by *Ko-ki* (mouth Reiki) blowing through pursed lips onto the burns.

[45] Yamaguchi, p. 125.

[46] Brown, p. 30.

[47] Yamaguchi, p. 10.

[48] Haberly, p. 58.

[49] Yamaguchi, p. 89.

Byosen[50]

Both Usui and Hayashi placed emphasis on the concept of *Byosen* and stressed developing sensitivity in the hands through practice, suggesting ways for students to accomplish this.

Byo translates as "ill, stiffness, toxic, or tumor"; *sen* translates as "gland, lump, block, or accumulation of toxins which disturb the flow of energy." The sensitive practitioner will receive messages from the recipient's body in the form of heat, cold, tingling, prickling, or other sensations in the hands. At times, the practitioner may feel discomfort in his or her own body that corresponds with the discomfort in the recipient's body. Focusing Reiki on the area of the body where *Byosen* is present helps to break down the toxins. The practitioner treats the area until the sensations ease or subside. *Byosen* may subside, and then peak two or three times during a 60–80-minute treatment.

Ketsueki Kokan Ho (Kekko)

A massage technique that increases circulation, purifies the blood and rejuvenates the body, *Kekko* is effective after a hands-on treatment and can also be practiced independently. Hayashi considered it an essential component of any Reiki treatment. It is a rather long and involved process with several steps that include stimulating the spine, the torso and legs in a specific pattern. Petter's book describes the process and provides detailed illustrations.[51] Caution should be exercised in using this technique, as many states in the US and some other countries require the practitioner to have a massage license to perform it.

Psychological Treatment

According to Yamaguchi, the term for the Mental/Emotional symbol indicated both the symbol, and a specific psychological treatment. He describes the method, which is to draw the Mental/Emotional symbol over the crown of the head, directing energy to the core of the brain. The practitioner then repeats phrases intended to reverse the negative habit. They are not affirmations, but rather admonitions using terms such as "must" or "mustn't" that give direct commands to the receiver's unconscious and conscious mind. Yam-

[50] The concept of Byosen is discussed in-depth in a three-part series, "Understanding Byosen Scanning," by Frank Arjava Petter, which appeared in the Spring, Summer, and Fall 2007 issues of *Reiki News Magazine*. See also *The Hayashi Reiki Manual*, p. 37–39, and *Light on the Origins of Reiki*, p. 73–76.

[51] Petter, p. 51–62.

aguchi believes this is more effective than the modern-day tendency for using positive affirmations. During the treatment, the practitioner may perceive sensations in the palms similar to *Byosen*; however, in this case it doesn't indicate an accumulation of toxins, but rather the flow of energy. Treatment is continued until the sensations ease or cease. The recipient may experience sensations as well—throbbing or a strong flow of energy in the head, tingling in the body, or at times may see a bright light.[52]

Enkaku (Distant Healing)

Distant Healing was not practiced frequently in Japan prior to World War II, as it was not as common then for family members to live at a distance from each other. This changed during the war when practitioners sent Reiki to those in the armed services.

Yamaguchi was taught that it is best to have a photograph of someone you have not met. It is important to visualize the person. If you don't know the person, get as much information as you can: full name, birth date or age, gender, and symptoms. Project the image of the recipient onto a part of your own body. Draw and say the *Enkaku Jumon*. Then place your hand on the area of your body that is the target area.[53]

I believe that knowledge of the techniques used in Japanese Reiki and information about the history of Reiki deepens our understanding and enriches our practice. We owe a tremendous debt of gratitude to Hayashi for his work in developing Reiki and for his willingness to allow this knowledge to spread to the West. Since Usui's *Gakkai* became a closed organization, it is unlikely that any of us in the West would know Reiki had Hayashi not formed his own institute. It is unlikely that Takata would have connected with the *Gakkai* in her search for healing, or if she had, that it would have agreed to admit her to the organization. And so, "Just for today," we can be grateful for the life and work of "diligent, warm-hearted" Chujiro Hayashi.

[52] Yamaguchi, p. 150.

[53] Ibid., p. 151.

Interview with Hiroshi Doi Sensei (2014)

BY WILLIAM LEE RAND

HIROSHI DOI SENSEI, a Gendai Ho Reiki Master who resides in Ashiya City, Japan, is a leading authority on the practice of Usui Reiki. His membership in the Usui Reiki Ryoho Gakkai places him in a unique position to access information about the style of Reiki developed and practiced by Usui Sensei. The Gakkai was the original organization started by Usui Sensei and the first four presidents of the organization through 1975 had received their Reiki training from him. Hiroshi Doi Sensei's access to the Shinpi-den members of the Gakkai including the two most recent presidents along with access to Gakkai archives gives him an authentic source of information. His devotion to Reiki and to researching and preserving the historical facts of its practice make him a valuable resource to the Reiki community. He has also developed a system of Reiki called *Gendai Reiki Ho* and authored a book, *Iyashino Gendai Reiki Ho, A Modern Reiki Method of Healing*. This book was first published in Japan in 1998 and in Canada in 2000, but it has been out of print for almost 10 years. Now a revised version has recently been published. This interview will focus on this book and especially on the new information that has been included. This is the first part of a two part interview. The answers for this interview were translated from Japanese by Fumi Koji.[1]

[1] A previous 2 part interview appeared in this magazine in 2003. "An Interview with Hiroshi Doi," *Reiki News Magazine*, Pts. 1 and 2 (Summer 2003): p. 9–11; (Fall 2003). http://www.reikimembership.com/articlesforms/hiroshidoiinterview.pdf

WLR: The revised edition of *Iyashino Gendai Reiki Ho, A Modern Reiki Method of Healing* has additional information important to the practice of Reiki as well as an improved translation that makes it easier for English speaking people to understand the esoteric concepts you have expressed. Can you describe some of the additional information that the revised edition includes?

HDS: This book was revised in Japanese in March 2008, 10 years after the first edition. But this revised edition in English is not merely a translation of the original. The translator, who is a Gendai Reiki Master, gave it a thorough examination, and made suggestions to upgrade the information, which she confirmed with me. Then, we reviewed the important concepts with you, William, knowing that with your worldwide knowledge as a Reiki Master with over 20 years experience, you would be able to help us express the information in a form that would be more easily understood by the Western mind.

Through this more detailed editing process, the book has grown to better convey the facts about Usui Reiki Ryoho with its purpose of health and happiness and to better explain Gendai Reiki Ho, which is a more compatible system for 21st century people to live by.

The revised edition contains some information that I had not made available to the public before as it would have been considered too sensational at that earlier time. However, the time is now right for this information to be released. For instance, in the book you will now read explanations of the fact that Dento Reiki (the Reiki Usui Sensei taught) has neither a fourth symbol (Master Symbol) nor any Kotodama (mantras) and that some of the requirements of the Shinpi-den level students of Usui Sensei's time have drastically changed since the time of the Gakkai's second president.

In general, this book explains as easily as possible what has become clear to me in more than 20 years of practicing and teaching Reiki Ho. My translator, Fumi Koji and and you William, wonderfully made this happen by sorting and drawing precise points out of the huge stack of archives inside me.

WLR: In the revised edition you explain that the entire healing system of Usui Reiki was taught by Usui Sensei in the Sho-den and Oku-den levels and that occasionally some of the Oku-den students were taught how to give reiju (attunements) and offered this to students. Could you explain how this took place?

HDS: The whole course of Reiki healing is taught in Sho-den and Oku-den in the Gakkai. When a member is given Oku-den Koki (the second half of Okuden), he/she is recognized as having completed the entire course of Usui Reiki healing. However, while the task of performing reiju is done by the Shihan (Shinpi-den title holder), some of those who were Oku-den Koki and in charge of local branches of the Gakkai were also taught reiju, and they offered this to the students of that branch. This took place only if the local branch didn't have a Shihan. Today, the Shihan from the head office will visit the branch to give reiju when the branch chief is not a Shihan.

WLR: You have also explained that the Gakkai have only three symbols, which are the same three that are taught in Western Reiki Level II. The Gakkai do not have a master symbol and there is no special reiju or attunement for those who become Shinpi-den. Was this always the case and is there any awareness, understanding or use of the Master DKM symbol by the Gakkai?

HDS: The third symbol is a unique shape that contains five kanji characters whose overlapping parts are removed. The meaning of the five kanji characters is: "The basics to become happy start with the right consciousness." This is the final symbol in the Gakkai's teachings; they do not have the fourth one. I confirmed this by asking Koyama Sensei (the sixth president), Kondo Sensei (the seventh president) and other Shihans, and they all said they did not know it.

Reiju is the method to let the internal Reiki of the person get tuned into the Universal Reiki. There is only one kind of reiju in the Gakkai and in Gendai Reiki Ho. Reiju it is not a technique to give special abilities; its only purpose is to open the "pipe" of Reiki. So there is no reiju for the beginners, reiju for advanced learners or reiju for Shinpi-den.

Gendai Reiki Ho employs the three kanji characters of DKM as the fourth symbol in its curriculum (Level III) knowing that it is not a part of Dento Reiki. It is used in Gendai Reiki Ho because it generates a high resonance effect with the sacred vibration and connects one with the Universal consciousness and brings this Light to our consciousness.

WLR: Some have said that the original purpose of Usui Reiki was for spiritual development, but that Usui Sensei eventually changed its purpose into a system of healing. How accurate is this statement? Could you clarify what the original purpose of Usui Reiki was and how it developed from the beginning to the present as practiced by the Usui Reiki Ryoho Gakkai?

HDS: Some groups claim that 臼井霊気療法 Usui Reiki Ryoho was intended to cure disease, as the Japanese word 療法 "ryoho" literally means the curing therapy. If so, Usui Reiki Ryoho would have been just another one of the treatment therapies that existed before Usui Sensei. Usui Sensei said, "I have never studied any methods for disease treatment." He also stated, "Usui Reiki Ryoho makes us fit and well, moderates our thought and enhances one's joy of life." and "Usui Reiki Ryoho heals Kokoro [mind and spirit] first, and then makes the body strong and healthy." These statements of his clearly mean that he did not give first priority to curing disease. Usui Sensei wrote two descriptive statements that introduce 五戒 Go-kai The Five Precepts: 招福の秘法 "Shofuku no Hiho" "The secret method to invite happiness" and the second one, 萬病の霊薬 "Manbyo no Reiyaku" "The miraculous remedy/elixir for all diseases" that follows it. In this way he indicates that the ultimate goal of Usui Reiki Ryoho is to become happy and that we enter this happy state by becoming healthy through hand healing. Gendai Reiki Ho summarizes these two titles as one: "The way to health and happiness." The point to remember is that Go-kai shows the same method for both happiness and health.

Usui Reiki Ryoho started from Usui Sensei's quest for the purpose of life. Healing and spiritual development are both like wheels that run one car, Usui Reiki. The axle that connects the wheels is the resonance with Reiki. However, at a time when most people in Japan were too poor to see a doctor or to buy medicine even if they were seriously sick, it was rather difficult to preach to them that they should understand Anshin Ritsumei (the purpose of life). Considering this social circumstance, Usui Sensei awakened public interest by using the name of "Reiki Ryoho" (medical treatment by Reiki) because the generic use of the word reiki (not necessarily connected with Usui Sensei) for healing was becoming popular at that time. Then he taught spiritual development to those who reached a certain level. He never changed the purpose of Usui Reiki Ryoho over the course of time.

WLR: Please explain the special spiritual training Usui Sensei provided for those students who were ready for the Shinpi-den level. Can you explain what that training consisted of and how long this training lasted for each student?

HDS: Usui Sensei had no standard curriculum, and the length of time of the training depended on the spiritual progress of each student. It is said that he gave one-on-one lectures mainly on the right mental attitude needed for spiritual advancement based on his own experience. As it was personal, only fragmentary notes of his words written by his student have been found. The note says:

"Everything in the Universe possesses Reiki without any exception." "We humans hold the Great Reiki that fills the Great Universe. The higher we raise the vibration of our own being, the stronger the Reiki we have inside will be.""The Natural Law of the Great Universe and each human spirit as a small universe must be constantly united and exist as One." "The Universe exists in me, and I exist in the Universe." "光明 Komyo exists in me and I exist in 光明 Kyomyo." [Komyo is the light of enlightenment.] "Everything in the universe is produced and developed by the magnificent Reiki that fills the Great Universe. Humans are a microcosm that takes the Great Spirit from macrocosm; everyone holds a part of this Great Reiki in his body. Therefore, we must always try to cultivate spirituality so that we can receive as much Great Reiki of the Universe as possible."

"The training according to the Natural Law of this whole world develops human spirituality. When you are convinced of this Truth, your committed training brings about the unification with the Universe. The words you speak and the actions you take become one with the Universe and they effortlessly work as the absolute limitlessness. This is the true nature of being human."

WLR: Can you give a more elaborate description of Anshin Ritsumei, the state of consciousness Usui Sensei received on Kurama Yama.

HDS: While experiencing a variety of occupations over the course of his life, Usui Sensei pondered the question as to whether there was a purpose of life and if there was, what was it. After a long quest, he came to the conclusion that the purpose of life was to become happy and happiness meant the attainment of the state of Anshin Ritsumei. He recognized Anshin Ritsumei as follows: "We humans are given life and a mission from the Universe. When it gives us life and a mission, it can never impose illness or misfortune on us. Regardless of what happens in life, we should trust the Universe and keep a peaceful mind state in order to accomplish our mission. This is the purpose and meaning of life." Though he logically comprehended what it should be, he was often perturbed by anger or fear in actual life. To experience that perfectly peaceful mind state, he practiced Zen meditation at a temple in Kyoto for three years. But it did not give him the true experience. He thought that he would not deserve to live any more if he could not attain the meaning of life. So he climbed Mt. Kurama for meditation and fasting with the readiness to die. He gradually felt that the Reiki inside him and the Reiki surrounding Mt. Kurama were vibrating with each other and that the vibration became stronger day by day. At midnight of the 21st day, a thunder-like shock hit him on the top of his head, and he lost consciousness. Then in the pre-dawn hours, he woke up to find himself filled with an amazing refreshment he had never felt before. "I am the Universe, the Universe is me!"It was the actual feeling of his soul in perfect resonance. Finally he was in the mind state he had longed for. It is said that from then on, he always kept that peace in his mind.

As he came joyfully down from the mountain, he tripped over a tree root and broke the left big toenail. He instinctively put his hand on it and it was cured immediately. This was the first of many healing experiences that occurred unexpectedly. He soon understood that healing took place through the resonance between his inner Reiki and Reiki of the Universe. He also recognized that the Universe had given him a mission to invite many people to find Anshin Ritsumei, the purpose of life, by way of a particular kind of hand healing. He named the method 心身改善臼井霊気療法 Shinshin Kaizen Usui Reiki Ryoho and established the Usui Reiki Ryoho Gakkai in Tokyo to provide both healing and training sessions for the general public.

WLR: To what extent was Usui Sensei able to help the Shinpi-den students attain Anshin Ritsumei?

HDS: It seems that he tried to create a certain and quick system to foster spiritual development for more people as he knew he would pass on soon. Many of them are said to have reached or nearly reached Anshin Ritsumei by studying with Usui Sensei. But I think that he was not satisfied with the personal lecture system as it could guide very few people to the purpose of life, to Anshin Ritsumei. Personal lectures are not always a guarantee of transmitting knowledge: they can be an effective method only if taught by the right person in the right way; thus its results will vary according to the instructor's competence and the student's readiness. I think Usui Sensei thought that he should provide a certain system and showed Ushida Sensei how to carry it out, as he put his trust in him. The system Usui Sensei handed down simply advised that one must have the right recognition of basic consciousness, that one must repeatedly engrave it into the subconscious mind and that one must enhance its resonance with the Universe. For this purpose, what Usui Sensei taught was based on a healing practice in which the student should strive for the unification with the Universe through regular practice of Go-kai and Hatsurei-ho, through reading the Gyosei of Emperor Meiji and through attendance at Shuyo-kai.

WLR: I understand that this special training was discontinued after Usui Sensei passed. Can you explain why it wasn't continued?

HDS: Usui Sensei's special lecture greatly strengthened and enhanced many of the Shinpi-den practitioners' spirituality. Furthermore, he seemed to try to create a certain and quick system to foster spiritual development for more numbers of people as he knew he didn't have a lot of time left in this life. I think he mentored the Shinpi-den practitioners so that the training would contribute to the spiritual advancement not only for the Shinpi-den practitioners but also for the rest of the Gakkai members. If Usui Sensei had intended to lead just a small cadre of elites to Anshin Ritsumei, he would not have needed to give them the responsibilities of board member and instructor. The lecture provided only to Shinpi-den practitioners was discontinued after Usui Sensei passed. I think it is much more natural to understand that this decision came about because they acknowledged Usui Sensei's intention that they must simply develop what they had learned with him.

WLR: You also explain that after Usui Sensei passed, the Gakkai offered no additional training for the Shinpi-den level—that it is honorary only, but does require those at this level to accept the responsibility of teaching others, managing the Gakkai and adding the finishing touch to the Oku-den practitioners healing treatments. It is also understood that those who are offered and accept the Shinpi-den level do not teach Reiki outside the Gakkai. Can you elaborate on the Shinpi-den level and give any additional details that may be important for us to know.

HDS: After Usui Sensei passed away, the Shinpi-den level changed and the healing practice became a method to directly encourage spiritual advancement. The main responsibility of the Shinpi-den today is to instruct the members as Shihan. They do not have to add the finishing touch to Okuden practitioners' healing treatments as members of the Gakkai do not provide healing sessions to the general public any more. They only give them to the members and their families. Now that they do not provide training sessions for the general public, the activity of the Shinpi-den practitioners is limited to activities inside the Gakkai. When an organization decreases in number, the number of board members decreases as well. As a result, very few of them are serving as board members now. None of the Shinpi-den, the Sho-den or Oku-den practitioners speak freely about Reiki outside the Gakkai like I, an Oku-den member, do, so I appreciate that this is my mission.

The more important thing to understand about Shinpi-den is that even if Usui Sensei had been alive today, it would have been very few who were assigned to his one-on-one lecture. Though the personal lecture for spiritual advancement is not available, Reiki still is the ubiquitous energy of the Universe that is available to guide and develop us. When we have this broader point of view, we can see that Usui Sensei's intention has been manifested; the system of spiritual learning that was reserved for Shinpi-den practitioners has only grown up to be available for everyone to receive its benefits. We also have to remember that we can get only what we have recognized. Although you may actually have a million dollars in your bag, if you believe you have just 500 dollars, you will be limited to making small purchases. If you believe Reiki cures only the body, "your Reiki" cures only the body. I think we should appreciate that Reiki is the energy of Love that guides us to Anshin Ritsumei and through the practice of Reiki healing we increase our trust in the Universe.

WLR: Gendai Reiki is a combination of Usui Reiki and Western Reiki and you have explained in your book that this is a style that is better suited for modern times. Could you please explain why it is better for modern times?

HDS: When we see the Reiki method as "the way of health and happiness," advantages and disadvantages of Western and Dento Reiki become clear to us. Western Reiki has had a focus on collecting medical evidence because its practitioners place priority on its healing effects. Dento Reiki, on the other hand, today considers the healing practice to be more on the level of home remedies and is not so interested in the scientific examination of its effects. The attitude of Western Reiki is validated by its historical background: Hayashi Sensei had developed the healing method according to his medical perspective and Takata Sensei first used Reiki to cure her diseases. She then learned Reiki from him and provided Reiki treatments into her later years at her clinic. Western Reiki had started from these two people. So it is quite natural that it emphasizes its use for healing treatments. But it seems that the importance of spiritual advancement, which is the basic philosophy of Usui Reiki Ryoho, was not exported to the West enough. When I spoke as a lecturer to introduce the true story of Usui Sensei and the contents of Dento Reiki at several workshops from 1999 in Vancouver to 2003 in Denmark, so many Reiki instructors wanted to know about the spiritual aspects. In that respect, Dento Reiki has a high level of spirituality regardless of whether the Gakkai members are aware of it or not.

Gendai Reiki Ho's way of health starts from the basic 12 hand positions of Western Reiki. But it is not merely a copy of the Western method. We employ the healing method in a way that encourages the healer's growth. Effective healing is important of course, but it must contribute to the spiritual development of the healer. Reiki healing heals both healer and healee at the same time. In the

Go-kai, the way of happiness refers to the spiritual aspect of Reiki practice and in Gendai Reiki Ho this is developed by having as its purpose the creation of a greater resonance between one's internal Reiki and Universal Reiki through the use of various methods. It will continue to develop its effectiveness to this end through the use of the motto: "Clear, practical and simple Reiki for daily use." I believe the combination of the healing aspect with the spiritual aspect is one of the biggest features of Gendai Reiki Ho.

Interview With Hiroshi Doi Sensei (2014) - Part II

This is the second part of a two-part interview. The first part appeared in the Spring 2014 edition of Reiki News Magazine. The answers for this interview were translated from Japanese by Fumi Koji.

WLR: What is the most important part of the Usui Reiki training?

HDS: After the first Reiju opens the Reiki "circuit" inside, we Reiki practitioners must strive to cleanse it to raise the quality and quantity of the energy that flows in the circuit. Also we must always keep the Kokoro (spirit or heart) in peace, being careful not to mix in negative energies, such as anger or fear.

The Usui Reiki Ryoho Gakkai puts special emphasis on the above, explaining in their terms: "To develop the pipe of Reiki." For this purpose, the Gakkai encourages its members to attend 修養会 Shuyo-kai, now called 研究会Kenkyu-kai (class), to receive Reiju as many times as possible, to exercise Hatsurei-ho (the exercise to accelerate Reiki flow), to consider the Gyosei (waka poems) of Emperor Meiji as food for Kokoro and to uphold Go-kai (the Five Reiki Principles).

Gendai Reiki Ho explains it this way: "To enhance the resonance of inner Reiki with the Universal Reiki." The practice of healing allows us to develop the pipe of Reiki, and it raises the purity of Reiki within us. The purer internal Reiki we have, the more resonance with the Universe we have. In this way, we get close to the complete oneness with the Universe. I believe this is the most important factor of Reiki practice.

WLR: What is the most important technique or skill to develop in Usui Reiki?

HDS: In 伝統霊気 Dento Reiki (based on the teachings of the Usui Reiki Ryo-ho Gakkai), after one has the Reiki circuit open and also continues to strive to raise the quantity and quality of the Reiki energy one is able to channel, it is important to learn how to use the Reiki energy. The most important skill in this respect is knowing where to place one's hands so one can provide an effective Reiki treatment. 病霊感法 Byosen Reikan-ho and 霊示法 Reiji-ho are the skills used to do this and are taught by the Gakkai on the first day of training. They are taught first because they are the most important and also because they take the most time in which to develop adequate skill.

Byosen is the negative energy that comes from an illness or area of distress in the client. It is detected by using the sensitivity in the hands. With ones hands in gassho one says prayers of gratitude for the healing that is about to take place and asks to be shown those areas in need of healing. Then the practitioner slowly moves the palm of the hand above the body of the client while paying attention to the sensations on the palm of the hand. When the practitioner detects a Hibiki (disturbance) on the palm of the hand, which is caused by byosen, the practitioner will begin to treat the area with Reiki. Reiji-ho uses one's Reiki guided intuition to know where to place the hands. It is done by placing ones hands into gassho and saying prayers of gratitude for the healing that is about to take place, and then asking to be directly shown where to place one's hands intuitively. This knowledge then enters the mind and the practitioner follows this guidance and places the hand on or over the area to be treated.

WLR: In the Gakkai, what is the usual length of time that a student takes to complete Sho-den and each of the levels of Oku-den?

HDS: It took me 10 years to complete as I was too busy at that time to attend Kenkyu-kai very often. There is no standard time duration since how long it takes depends on the development of a person's healing ability. The Gakkai says that some take only five years and some take more than 20 years. There were 21 who were learning Shinpi-den from Usui Sensei at the time of his passing. As Usui Sensei lived for only four years after he started the Gakkai, it is assumed that his students might have taken about two or three years to learn Sho-den, Oku-den Zenki and Oku-den Koki. Compared with those outstandingly advanced people, it is reasonable that general practitioners now need more time.

WLR: How do the Shinpi-den teachers determine when a student has completed the Usui Reiki training and is ready to receive his or her certificate?

HDS: Which Shihan instructs a class changes depending on the day, and the students can choose freely whose training to take. All the Shihans know the ability of the students who earnestly choose to come to Kenkyu-kai and training sessions. The student's ability is carefully checked when he or she is willing to go on from Sho-den to Oku-den level. 師範会Shihan-kai, a meeting attended by Shihans only, is held several times a year to discuss the competence of the student(s). The Shihans must all be in agreement in order to declare that a student has completed the training. It is voted down even if only one Shihan disagrees. If they all agree on the choice of a particular student, they issue the certificate, which is signed by the president.

WLR: Did Usui Sensei include any additional training for the use of Reiki as a healing method in the Shinpi-den level or was the content only about spiritual development?

HDS: When a member finishes Oku-den Koki, the Gakkai issues a certificate that acknowledges that he/she has completely fulfilled the healing ability requirements of Usui Reiki Ryoho. There was even a time when the Gakkai issued the equivalent of a special certificate to be able to charge for healing sessions.

Usui Sensei did not give additional healing trainings but I heard that he often taught classes about a Shihan's mental attitude in order to improve one's teaching methods when teaching about healing to the members. Though his one-on-one Shinpi-den lecture did not include healing training, I also heard that Usui Sensei's mentorship greatly enhanced the healing ability of many of the Shinpi-den practitioners, as it strengthened their resonance with the Universe and encouraged the awareness that a human is the small universe derived from the Great Universe.

WLR: You mention that you developed Gendai Reiki as a system of healing for your own personal use and then when people commented on how much healthier you looked you decided to teach it to others. Could please you comment on how this developed?

HDS: I am familiar with 座禅 Zazen (seated Zen meditation) and therefore even early on, the invisible world was quite natural for me to understand. After finishing school, I worked for a national telephone company and moved to one of the biggest automobile companies after 12 years. And after that I changed jobs often. I was very short-tempered when I was young. When things did not turn out to be what I had expected, I became furious and at the same time I was disturbed by fear. I was on a roller coaster ride of emotion. I even lost a chance to join a company that had just accepted me under advantageous conditions as I had a tussle with the new boss at the welcome party for me.

At a certain point in my life, I became interested in healing because my best friend was suffering from an incurable disease. I learned more than 30 types of healing methods and one of them was Reiki. I first learned Western Reiki, and had a gut feeling that this was what I had wanted to find. People said that the traditional Usui Reiki Ryoho and the Gakkai were gone. But I knew otherwise, since I happened to know of the existence of the Gakkai. I joined them through an old member. In October 1993, the sixth president, Kimiko Koyama Sensei, gave me my first Reiju at the Kyoto branch, and I could not stop the tears that came because of a kind of homecoming feeling that went through me. As I continued to practice Reiki, I realized that a peaceful mind state was gradually returning, and I expected that my episodes of short-temper would soon lessen. Around this time, valuable information of Usui Sensei's times came to me quite naturally through conversations with my acquaintances. I sorted this information out to construct an effective and practical Reiki system to continue to improve myself. Gendai means modern; Gendai Reiki Ho is the way to practice Reiki for modern people. I have kept developing it to be a more effective system according to my studies and trials. I developed Gendai Reiki Ho in order to improve myself, and my short temper completely disappeared without my even realizing it. Then people who noticed my change asked me to teach them. In this way, it has become popular quite naturally.

WLR: In Gendai Reiki the Reiju or attunements are not the same as that given by Usui Sensei or the Gakkai. Please explain how you developed this attunement method and why you chose to do so.

HDS: Gendai Reiki Ho's attunements are based on Neo Reiki in the lineage of Osho Reiki, which included fairly accurate information about Dento Reiki. I think its attunement method is simpler and more effective than any other of the Reiki methods.

Gendai-Reiju is an original Reiju method that quickly attunes one to the Reiki wavelength. It is a different method from that of Dento Reiki today.

Around the time of the Gakkai's establishment, Usui Sensei, using his wisdom and ingenuity, modified the Reiju methods many times to make them more effective. Gendai-Reiju is based on one of the earlier methods he developed.

WLR: In your Gendai Reiki Master Reiju you use the Master DKM symbol, even though it isn't used by the Gakkai nor was it used in Dento Reiki. Could you please explain why you have chosen to do this and the value of doing so.

HDS: The Gendai Reiki Ho Master attunement integrates all four symbols to produce a new Reiki Master. Most Western Reiki schools attune students to the three symbols in the second level and the fourth symbol in the third or Master level. I refer to this as "setting" the symbols in the practitioner's energy body. Those symbols can sometimes be set without balancing each other. When the four symbols are set properly, the practitioner can use each one without any trouble. But when some of these symbols do not balance each other, the effect isn't as great as could be expected from their combined use. I know from my experience that about 60% of Master students have the four symbols in good balance. In these cases, the Gendai Reiki Ho Master attunement has no effect one way or the other. However, in the case of the other 40%, when the four symbols are not balanced amongst themselves, this attunement provides that balance, and it will remain permanently. The purpose of this integrating attunement is to produce a new Master with balance among the four symbols.

WLR: What do you see as the future of your work with Reiki?

HDS: I will turn 80 November 2, 2015, so I am not going out of my way to advertise my seminar; however I am pleased to continue to support Reiki practitioners while I still have my health and my mission. My main activity is to be advisory support for the Gendai Reiki Network (GRN), which is a non-profit organization that is managed voluntarily by a group of Gendai Reiki practitioners, my fellow classmates of Light. The GRN provides all of us with opportunities to teach and learn from each other as well as to promote Reiki in the right way. GRN offers free healing sessions and hosts Koryu-kai that anyone can attend in major cities throughout Japan. It also organizes a Reiki retreat and 研鑽会 Kensan-kai (study meeting) and works cooperatively with a physician in studying medical evidence of Reiki treatments.

The international network of Gendai Reiki has been sprouting up in many countries, growing with the GRN to exchange deep friendships. This movement has increased since the five-day event in Kyoto on March 2012, with many Gendai Reiki practitioners attending from abroad. In March 2014, we had 交流会 Koryu-kai (gathering/sharing) in Kyoto with Spanish- and English-speaking practitioners. When foreign practitioners visit Japan to join the GRN events, I arrange the Master Special Course to help them develop a clear understanding of Reiki. I expect to have more chances to bring foreign practitioners to Japan to share in new friendships and exchanges with Japanese practitioners.

An Interview with Hiroshi Doi (2003)

BY WILLIAM LEE RAND

HIROSHI DOI is a leading authority on the practice of Reiki in Japan. His membership in the Usui Reiki Ryoho Gakkai places him in a unique position to access information about the original Reiki methods of Dr. Mikao Usui. His dedication to healing and to preserving the Usui system of Reiki makes him a valuable resource to the Reiki community. He has also developed a system of Reiki Ryoho called Gendai Reiki and is the author of Iyashino Gendai Reikiho, Modern Reiki Method for Healing. He resides in Kyoto, Japan. This is the first part of a two part interview. This article was translated from Japanese by Hyakuten Inamoto.

William: ***Can you explain your background that led you to Reiki? Did you study other healing methods or meditation techniques before getting involved with Reiki?***

Doi Sensei: My grandfather was a Zen Buddhist monk and his lineage went back generation after generation. I did not become a Zen monk, but I practiced Zazen (sitting meditation) since childhood and, in a natural way, believed in the world of the unseen. After graduation I worked for the then government-run telephone company and left the company after 12 years. Since then I have had many careers. During those days I kept practicing Zazen (not so enthusiastically, though).

I think I was unconsciously seeking after my life purpose. The reason why I changed my career often was because I found each job to be inappropriate for my life purpose.

I know now that what matters more is how to deal with a job and what to learn from the job rather than what kind of job to take. I guess I was chasing after the Blue Bird of Happiness outside myself.

My family members and I have been gifted with good health, but there were many colleagues and customers of the company who suffered from intractable diseases. A good friend of mine became paralyzed on one side of the body due to cerebral hemorrhage, and this incident made me interested in "healing." Without knowing it I became very much absorbed in healing things and I learnt more than 30 different healing modalities during the 80's and 90's in hopes of opening up a healing salon at my house when I reached the age of 60.

During the early stage of my healing studies I happened to make the acquaintance of a person who was a traditional Japanese Reiki practitioner. However, at the time I had no idea he was a Reiki practitioner. I was just told that it was an effective hands-on healing method. I might have an opportunity later on to detail this story.

William: ***When did you first hear about Reiki and when did you take your first Reiki class? Can you give us some of the details such as who were your first teachers etc.?***

Doi Sensei: It was about the end of the 80's when I first heard the name "Reiki" in a Tokyo conscious energy workshop called "Shinmeikan healing". One of the participants had a book titled Reiki Ryoho which was a Japanese version of The Reiki Factor written by Dr. Barbra Ray and translated by Ms. Mieko Mitsui, a New York resident. Ms. Mitsui is a Reiki Teacher of the Radiance Technique and I heard she was back in Japan holding Reiki seminars. I attended her 1st and 2nd Degree Reiki classes in Osaka. This was 1990 or 1991.

When I joined the 1st Degree class I was suffering from pain in my left wrist caused by an excessive practice of golf and I could hardly sleep at night. To my surprise my pain was healed overnight. It was at my first experience of Reiki and it was at this time that I first became aware of Reiki.

William: ***What were the events that lead to you being invited to be a Gakkai member? (Gakkai means organization and refers to the Reiki organization started by Usui Sensei - The Usui Reiki Ryoho Gakkai)***

Doi Sensei: I had the 2nd Degree Reiki training with Ms. Mitsui and I was very willing to learn the 3rd Degree having heard that spiritual uplift could be boosted up with the 3rd Degree Reiki. As I have no knowledge of any foreign language, I was hoping to learn Reiki in Japan. Ms. Mitsui was not qualified to teach classes above the 3rd Degree, so I had to content myself with the 2nd Degree at the time.

I was told that traditional Japanese Reiki had become extinct and that the Gakkai no longer existed, but I was wondering, even though Gakkai was gone, there must have been some students who were the members of a Gakkai branch as Gakkai had branch offices all over Japan, and I wanted to learn Reiki from them. I tried to gather helpful information via the Internet and other means, but in vain. Thus, I arrived at the conclusion that the Gakkai had completely vanished.

In the summer of '93 I went to Tokyo to attend a British style crystal healing seminar. There I happened to pair off with an old lady who had been a Gakkai member for more than 40 years. From her I learned that the Usui Reiki Ryoho Gakkai still existed. Thanks to an introduction by her, I was invited to become a member of the Gakkai in October, 1993. In Kyoto I was newly initiated into Reiki by Mrs. Koyama, the 6th President, in due form of traditional Reiki Ryoho Reiju (Gakkai style attunement). Koyama Sensei was 87 years old at the time and I vividly recall that she was kind enough to allow a new member like me to sit next to her and responded tenderly to many questions of mine.

William: ***I understand that the Gakkai was started by Dr. Usui. Can you tell us about its history? How was it started and how did it develop? Who were the important people? How did it change because of the war etc.? Please include any interesting facts or details.***

Doi Sensei: Usui Sensei was born in August 1865 in Taniai-mura, a village in Gifu-ken prefecture. He left his hometown at an early age and struggled throughout his studies in Europe, America, and China. He broadened his ideas through many different careers: public servant, office worker, businessman, newspaperman, secretary, and politician, among others. Eventually he came to seek the purpose of life and to recognize that the purpose of life is to attain the state of an-shin ritsu-mei, that is, to learn the fact that man has been given a role to play that is sustained by the universe and then to fulfill one's role with a calm mind by trusting and leaving all to the universe, no matter what happens in the course of life. He set upon the path of Zen Buddhism in order to grasp that meaning as a real feeling in his soul, not as a mere comprehension in his head. At a Buddhist temple in Kyoto, he trained himself in Zazen meditation for about three years to strive for a true state of satori, or enlightenment, like an-shin ritsu-mei. But a state of satori still eluded him.

In the spring of 1922 on Kurama-yama, he set out to fast with the resolve that his life would end there unless he attained enlightenment. At midnight on the 21st day of his fast, a strong Reiki of the universe penetrated his brain, resonating with Reiki in his body, and he attained a feeling of oneness with the universe. He was then enlightened and, at the same time, a healing power was bestowed upon him. Usui Sensei named it Reiki Ryoho and decided not to monopolize it, but to share it with many people. He created the principles, or Five Precepts, and the instructional method. He moved to Aoyama, in Tokyo, and founded the Usui Reiki Ryoho Gakkai.

Enrollment as a member was required because a prescribed instruction was necessary to learn Reiki Ryoho, but Reiki treatments were offered to non-members. People from all over who wanted treatments waited in long lines outside the house. Many high-ranking naval officers were enrolled in the Gakkai. One of them was Rear Admiral Ushida Juzaburo, who became the second president of the Gakkai and the successor of Usui Sensei. Rear Admiral Taketomi Kanichi took office as the third president and Vice Admiral Wanami Hoichi, as the fifth president, administered the Gakkai in a difficult postwar time.

Naval Captain Hayashi Chujiro, who enrolled later, accomplished an important role: to spread Reiki the world over, thus meeting Usui Sensei's expectations.

In September 1923 the Great Kanto Earthquake occurred. It was a great disaster, with 104,000 people killed or missing and 460,000 homes collapsed or destroyed by fire. Usui Sensei and his disciples roved the town the days following the quake, treating the wounded and saving innumerable people from death. It is said that this incident brought more new members— writers, entertainers, religious men, and martial arts practitioners to the Gakkai. In February 1925, the new dojo of the Gakkai was built in Nakano in order to expand the Gakkai. From this time on, Usui Sensei was frequently invited to teach and treat people all over the country.

In March1926 he suddenly passed away on the road in Fukuyama. It is said that Usui Sensei had over 2,000 students and 21 of them were given Shinpiden. The names of eleven Shinpiden students, three of them women, are being confirmed.

William: ***Is the Gakkai the only group or school that is teaching the original form of Usui Reiki Ryoho or are there others?***

Doi Sensei: Strictly speaking, the Gakkai is the only group (organization) that continues to use the original form of Usui Reiki Ryoho (philosophy and techniques). People who left the Gakkai, (mentioned in the second interview) presumably continued with the energy of Usui Reiki Ryoho, but structured an original style of their own by adding new ideas or casting aside things traditional. There are some people in Japan and in the West who claim, "this (mine or ours) is the original form of Usui Reiki Ryoho." This claim should be fairly inspected and verified.

The Gakkai has preserved the original form putting a strong stress on its mission to continue teaching the tradition of Usui Sensei, which has made the Gakkai appear exclusive from the outside. I've been suggesting that they (the Gakkai) should make efforts to realize another mission assigned by Usui Sensei that "Reiki Ryoho should be shared with many people and the joy be jointly shared

William: ***Can you explain what your training was like in the Gakkai? What did you learn as a new member and what took place at the meetings?***

Doi Sensei: During Usui Sensei's time the meeting was called the Shuyokai. It is now called Kenkyu-kai and is held at the Tokyo head office three times a month. Because of my job, I was unable to attend the Tokyo meetings and instead joined those held at the Kyoto branch. At that time, Koyama Sensei would come to Kyoto almost every month. Senior members encouraged me to sit next to Koyama Sensei, saying, "As you are a new member, sit near Koyama Sensei so that you will receive a lot of Reiki."

At Kenkyu-kai, Seiza-style sitting was once the practice, but now participants sit on chairs in a circle. The meetings began with talks by Koyama Sensei. The talks were not serious ones, but on a variety of topics based on Koyama Sensei's own experiences. I recognized that, on the whole, her talks embraced many lessons on how to live in peace through the guidance of Reiki. After her talks, Gyosei of the Meiji Emperor are recited. Then Kenyoku, Joshin-kokyu, Gassho, and Seishin-to-itsu are performed. Next all the participating members receive Reiju, (attunement) which is given by Koyama Sensei and a Shihan, who is appointed each time by Koyama Sensei. After Reiju, the Five Precepts are recited three times, followed by Reiji; then there is a question and answer session, Reiki-mawashi, and finally Shuchu-Reiki.

William: ***Did you receive any special training from Mrs. Koyama?***

Doi Sensei: Koyama Sensei used to say, "Reiki is the light of love," and that it is important to give hands-on treatments with one's heart wishing to be helpful to many people. I had an opportunity to receive hands-on treatments from Koyama

Sensei several times. The treatments were carefully and comfortably done. She used to tell me often, "Look, this is Hibiki." Being able to sense Byosen (Hibiki) is the very basis of traditional Reiki Ryoho.

William: ***Can you please explain Hibiki.***

Doi Sensei: When there is a life energy block or a disturbance in health, there are always minus waves (negative waves) in the causal area. They are called "Byosen" and the technique to sense Byosen in the hands is called "Byosen Reikan Ho". And "hibiki" is a sensation in your palms when Byosen is detected. These can include a variety of sensations such as heat, cool, painfulness, numbness (tingle) and the like varying from healer to healer. Hibiki occurs at the spot of the cause of the disease, not at the symptom area. For instance, in the case of a headache "hibiki" occurs on the head if the cause lies in the brain, but there will be no "hibiki" on the head if the cause lies in an internal organ.

Also, if there is a cause there will be "hibiki" even before a symptom of the disease appears. Even after a doctor declares "a complete recovery" there is a high probability of relapse while "hibiki" remains. It is necessary to get rid of it (hibiki) in order for a complete recovery to take place.

William: ***How long did it take to become an Okuden (Reiki II)? What were the requirements to graduate to this level?***

Doi Sensei: It took me seven years. I received Shoden (Reiki I) on October 22, 1993 and officially received Okuden on October 28, 2000. In traditional Reiki Ryoho, basics of Teate-Ryoho (hands-on method) are perfected at the Shoden level. New enrollees are given Shoden after they receive the first Reiju and are then certified at 6 Toh, or 6th rank, in capability. After this point, their rank is upgraded according to the progress they make in their training. One is certified as 3 Toh, or 3rd rank, when one successfully completes the foundations of Teate-Ryoho. The abilities to be mastered to attain this rank are sensing Byosen (Hibiki) exactly, followed by performing Reiji, in which one's hands are guided and naturally led to Byosen, and finally having it recognized that one's capabilities of Teate-Ryoho, or radiant Reiki power, have surpassed a certain norm.

Those who are certified at 3 Toh can move on to Okuden if they desire, but without application for the Okuden level the member remains at the Shoden level. As Usui Sensei graded himself at 2 Toh, or 2nd rank, the highest rank among members is the 3rd rank. Shinpiden members stay on the same level with Okuden members in terms of their capacity.

William: ***Can you explain the Okuden level? What did you learn and what skills did you develop?***

Doi Sensei: As I mentioned in response to the previous question, Shoden is the level at which one perfects the basic skills of Reiki Ryoho. The treatment or healing at this level is mainly intended for oneself and one's family members. At the Okuden level the benefits of Reiki are to be shared with many people. When there were 60 branches of the Gakkai offering Reiki Ryoho training to anyone who desired it, it was the Okuden members who were the healers.

Now Reiki Ryoho treatments at the Gakkai are limited to Gakkai members and their families because of medical system regulations. Traditional techniques like osu (pressing), naderu (stroking) and tataku (patting) are no longer practiced for fear that such techniques would be considered massage and no longer conform to laws and regulations. Only techniques of sensing Byosen and hands-on treatment are taught now, though at the Okuden level, the three symbols and mantras are taught in the name of tradition, to be handed down.

The techniques I teach at my seminars or workshops are not those of the current Usui Reiki Ryoho Gakkai, but chiefly those from the time of Usui Sensei to Wanami Sensei.

An Interview With Hiroshi Doi (2003) - Part II

William: ***Can you explain something about the Okuden symbols? Is the Gakkai understanding of the symbols different than our understanding in the West and can you explain this?***

Doi Sensei: The three symbols, if one is strictly speaking, are different from those used in the West. The symbols used in the West do vary a little from each lineage or school, but they are still not completely deviating and, on the whole, look very much the same as the traditional ones. The traditional symbols differ slightly in shape, though we may call them different from those of the West.

The symbols are effective tools in Reiki and, in my opinion, have two roles. The first role is to connect the practitioner to the special frequency of Reiki waves specific to each symbol. The second use of the symbols is to alter the length of the waves according to the practitioner's purpose or purposes so that the higher waves of Reiki can be utilized on earth. For instance, the first symbol is used like a transformer when more Reiki "power" is needed. Moreover, the more people use the symbol, the more effective it becomes, due to the accumulation of collective consciousness. I think that the symbols, because they are easy to use and because of their effectiveness, greatly help in the spread of Reiki.

However, Usui Sensei said, "You will find for yourself that you have no need of the symbols after you have used them again and again and again," and you will soon "uplift your consciousness to become one with the universe." So even though the symbols are tools to connect with Reiki, their necessity will no longer exist when everything in your daily life comes to resonate with Reiki.

I compare the symbols to a rubber swimming tube used when one first learns to swim. The tube is a very helpful tool for a beginner, but one needs to let go of it to become good at swimming. Up to the point at which one no longer needs them, the symbols, like the rubber tube, should be used with care. But if one believes that one's abilities are owing to the tool, one will not be able to let go of it. The basis of the symbol is the same all over the world, though some differences between the symbols themselves can be found; in the same way that rubber swimming tubes vary a little in their design, if not their purpose.

William: *Would you please give a description for each of these Japanese Reiki concepts:*

Doi Sensei:

Byosen: This is negative energy that occurs at the area of the cause of a disorder or disease.

Kenyoku: Traditionally a body is cleansed with water before performing sacred rituals, and Kenyoku is a purification method to cleanse a body with Reiki energy in place of water.

Joshin-kokyu: This is a breathing method to purify the mind.

Gassho: This is done by placing the hands together in front of one's breast to express gratitude or to say a prayer.

Seishin-to-itsu: This a meditation method used to calm the mind and let go of idle/stray thoughts.

Reiju: This is the original form of Japanese attunement.
Reiki-mawashi: Students stand in a circle holding hands and allow Reiki energy to flow around the circle.
Shuchu-Reiki: This is done in a group with hands in Gassho. The students focus their consciousness on one thing such as a person, an object, an event, a venue, etc., and the Reiki energy of all the practitioners is concentrated on the object. Shuchu-Reiki can be done when we pray for the world peace or for health and happiness.

William: ***Is there anything interesting about the Gakkai and its teachings that you think important for us in the West to know?***

Doi Sensei: It seems there are rumors that the *Gakkai* is exclusive and reluctant to accept people, that those who have learned Western Reiki will be excluded, or that foreign people in particular are excluded. If these rumors were true I may well have already been expelled from the Gakkai myself. I have never concealed the fact of my having learned Western Reiki and *Shinpiden* and *Okuden* practitioners from the *Gakkai* freely come and join my Reiki Gathering.

On the other hand, it is true that there are some among the senior members who are not happy with my activities outside the *Gakkai*. This kind of thing happens everywhere. I believe that all I need to do is just do my part. I heard that a foreign lady once met with Koyama Sensei just before leaving Japan, and that she was very moved to hear Koyama Sensei say, "You could be a member and learn if you would stay here longer." Koyama Sensei was very thoughtful and all embracing, and I think because she was so, she had no intention to exclude people.

Yet it is true that the *Gakkai* has shrunken in size and has not established a system to enroll many new members. This is because Koyama Sensei, having assumed office as the first female president at the time of turmoil after the war, was very busy struggling to preserve the light of tradition that was, at many points in time, on the edge of ruin, as people showed no interest in Reiki. This may have resulted in the *Gakkai* appearing to be exclusive from an outside point of view.

At the New Year meeting at the *Gakkai* Head Office in January of 2001, Mr. Kondo, the current president, asked me to tell to him and the other *Shihan* (teachers) about the state of Reiki in the West. They all expressed a strong interest. I proposed that the *Gakkai* could offer information on the *Gakkai* website. But they were not ready for that, and the proposal was declined.

Later, I asked for a message from the president to be delivered at the URRI Spain 2001 meeting, but in vain. However, Kondo Sensei does say to the members whenever he has an opportunity, "Let's uplift ourselves so that we do not feel ashamed in the face of Reiki people in the West."

On a New Year's greeting card from Kondo Sensei this year he wrote, "I feel happy to learn that Reiki is being globally recognized." Usui Sensei voiced this wish for the future: "I'd like to share a joy in common with many people by teaching them Reiki Ryoho." I believe that wish will be realized, and that everybody will be able to touch Usui Sensei's energy.

William: *What role did Dr. Hayashi play in the Gakkai?*

Doi Sensei: It is said that Hayashi Chujiro Sensei was the last *Shinpiden* disciple certified by Usui Sensei and was *Shihan*. At the time a *Shinpiden* disciple was supposed to engage in the spread of *Reiki Ryoho* and in Reiki treatments at the *Gakkai* head office or to open branch offices and engage in Reiki activities. Usui Sensei assigned a task to Hayashi Sensei, who was a naval doctor, to open a Reiki clinic apart from the *Gakkai* activities, in order to study and promote the efficacy of *Reiki Ryoho* from a medical doctor's point of view. Of course, it was intended for the results to feed back to the *Gakkai*.

William: *I understand that he broke away from the Gakkai to form his own school. Can you tell us why he did this?*

Doi Sensei: *Hayashi Reiki Kenkyu Kai* is said to have started at the time Hayashi Sensei opened the clinic, not at the time he left the *Gakkai*. The role of Hayashi Sensei was "to cure many of the sick by means of Reiki treatments," and "to study to improve the efficacy of *Reiki Ryoho* through treatments." His clinic's purpose was to accomplish this former goal and the latter one resulted in the organization of *Hayashi Reiki Kenkyu Kai*. Neither of these activities was part of the *Gakkai*, but was set up through Usui Sensei, though both seemed to have been initiated with the full support of the Gakkai.

It was after Usui Sensei's transition, or death, that Hayashi Sensei became independent as *Hayashi Reiki Kenkyu Kai* and left the *Gakkai*. Supposedly, there were differences of opinion between then President Ushida and Hayashi Sensei. It appears that a policy allowing Hayashi Sensei to study freely was changed. Hayashi Sensei, after having become independent as

Hayashi Reiki Kenkyu Kai, respected Usui Sensei and kept handing down Usui Sensei's teachings and the name of *Usui Reiki Ryoho* to people. He did this by practicing Reiki treatments and teaching classes with a scroll hanging in the front of the room, written by Hayashi Sensei himself, bearing the Five Precepts—*Usui Mikao Sensei Ikun Gokai*—an admonition of the late Usui Mikao Sensei. The same three-level system as the *Gakkai*, with *Shoden*, *Okuden*, and *Shinpiden* levels, was adopted. Certificates issued are under the name of *Hayashi Reiki Kenkyu Kai*, but they carry the name *Shinshin Kaizen Usui Reiki Ryoho* or Mind/Body Improvement Usui Reiki Ryoho, to signify that *Usui Reiki Ryoho* is instructed.

William: *How did Dr. Hayashi's style of Reiki change after he left the Gakkai?*

Doi Sensei: It is not that his style changed when he left the *Gakkai*, but that a new style was developed from the beginning of his *Kenkyu Kai*.

A recipient, except a seriously ill person, was to sit when receiving treatment; this sitting position was changed to a lying position on a table. The treatment method was changed from one-on-one to several-on-one.

These are the most outstanding features of the change, but the following changes are also recognized:

An original hands-on position was developed and the new *Reiki Ryoho Shinshin* or "Guidelines for Reiki Healing Method" were created. A new system of conferring and passing on *Reiki Ryoho* was established, and a monthly five-day workshop was held at which *Okuden* was given.

While at the *Gakkai*, the navel and the Tanden were considered important, the energy centers like the meridian lines of acupuncture, *Tsubo*, or vital points, and charka, etc. became important.

William: *Were there any other members who broke away from the Gakkai and started their own schools of Reiki similar to what Dr. Hayashi did?*

Doi Sensei: It's said that at the time of Mr. Ushida's presidency many members broke away. The following two that are well known:

Mr. Eguchi Toshihiro learned *Reiki Ryoho* from 1925 to 1927. Critical of the *Gakkai*, he became independent, and set up *Tenohira Ryochi Kenkyu Kai*. Well known among his students were Mr. Eguchi Yasukiyo, Mr. Mitsui Koshi, and Mr. Miyazaki Goro. It is estimated that there were 500,000 students under him.

Mr. Tomita Kaiji learned *Reiki Ryoho* from around 1925 and set up *Teate Ryoho Kai* after Usui Sensei's death. He propagated *Tomita-ryu Teate Ryoho*. There were four levels: *Shoden*, *Chuden*, *Okuden*, and *Kaiden*. Each level was to be completed in five days with two hours' training each day, but fifteen days were required to complete Kaiden. Famous among his students was Mr. Asuke Jiro. It's estimated that there were over 200,000 students.

Besides the two people mentioned above, it's said that there were several people who established new organizations or became religious men, but this is denied by each organization involved. Only Hayashi Sensei kept handing down the name of *Usui Reiki Ryoho* in respect for Usui Sensei, even after he had broken away from the *Gakkai*.

William: *Can you explain Gendai Reiki and why you decided to create it?*

Doi Sensei: *Gendai Reiki Ho*, or Gendai Reiki, based on Usui Sensei's philosophy and the rationality of Western Reiki, is designed to be easily practiced in daily life and with maximum benefits. It is not "a new *Reiki Ryoho*", nor is it "a new Reiki lineage", but it is "the new method to practice *Reiki Ryoho*", which I've been practicing for myself and of which I have been enjoying the benefits all of the time.

How Gendai Reiki Ho was created

I learned Western Reiki and acknowledged that it is highly effective. Later, I was initiated into Reiki by Koyama Sensei, president of the *Gakkai*, and I really felt the lofty spirituality handed down from Usui Sensei. Since then, I came by valuable materials and information about Reiki. I sorted and structured them with a focus on "mind/body healing" and "spiritual growth" so that I could benefit from it myself. That is what is called *Gendai Reiki Ho*. At first I was practicing it alone, but my friend who had become aware of a change in me asked that I hold a seminar for three therapists. That was the impetus for spreading it to people who were drawn to me. We have been striving together to grow ever since.

Usui Sensei said, "Reiki is Ki (energy) and Light that fills the universe." Reiki are waves of light that lead all to harmony, and fill the space all around us. In order to receive Reiki, it is necessary that a receiving set is completed. The techniques of *Gendai Reiki Ho* are those of "self-purification and self-development' that aim at resonance with Reiki waves all of the time, with no consciousness required after completion of a receiving set, but with lots of conscious practices of the techniques.

It is not their purpose merely to be learned and used.

The basic points of Gendai Reiki Ho

Gendai Reiki Ho was structured based on the following four premises:

1. "Mind/body healing" and "spiritual growth" are the key words. These are techniques that allow one to live life abundantly.

2. Effectiveness is stressed. Dogmatism, prejudice and secrecy should be avoided.

3. Secret, mystery and miracle are not advocated.

4. Effective techniques that promote characteristics of Reiki should be adopted. The purpose and reason should be clarified.

5. Techniques should be simplified, standardized and easily used. Use in daily life comes first.

William: *Is Gendai Reiki considered to be Japanese Reiki or is it a combination of Japanese and Western Reiki?*

Doi Sensei: Gendai Reiki Ryoho can be considered to be Japanese Reiki seen from the perspective of "the energy", but seen from that of "the use" it is a combination of Japanese and Western. However, from a standpoint of efficacy for "mind/body healing" and "spiritual growth", the techniques are adopted not only from Japanese Reiki or Western Reiki, but also from other than Reiki Ryoho. In Japan Gendai Reiki is being understood that it is a simplified Japanese Reiki for modern people with an addition of rationality (practicality) of Western Reiki.

Origin of the Usui Reiki Master Symbol

BY WILLIAM LEE RAND

THE USUI DKM MASTER SYMBOL is something most Western Usui Reiki Masters are aware of and use in their Reiki practice. It's used when giving Reiki sessions and is also an important part of the attunement process. Until recently, the fact that it is a part of Usui Reiki was never questioned, but in the past several years information has surfaced from reliable sources that tells a different story.

The history and practice of Western Usui Reiki has taken many twists and turns over the years. Takata Sensei presented one version of the history, which for a long time wasn't questioned. But starting in the 1990s and proceeding to the present day, research has taken place that has uncovered the fact that her story was filled with inaccuracies. The biography she told of Usui Sensei including why and how he discovered Reiki was the first to fall. Then we learned that the style of Reiki taught by Takata Sensei wasn't the same as that taught by Usui Sensei or Hayashi Sensei. This article will focus on the Usui DKM Master symbol, explaining its origin and when it came into use as a Reiki symbol. There will also be information about who introduced it, including a possible explanation as to why it was introduced.

This is another article in a series of articles on an evidence based history of Reiki. The research methods involved in this series are those used by professional historical researchers and are described in the article, *An Evidence Based History of Reiki*, which appeared in the Fall 2013 issue of *Reiki News Magazine* and was also in the December 2013 issue of the *Reiki Online Newsletter*.[1]

The DKM has its origin as a Japanese Buddhist mantra that is drawn in kanji ideograms. It can be translated to have several slightly different meanings such as *Great Bright Light, the Light of Wisdom by which illumination dawns on us, a brilliant enlightened aura*[2] and the Zen Buddhists translate it to mean *treasure house of the great beaming light.*[3] It is used by various Buddhist groups and other religious organizations in Japan to express an important spiritual concept.

[1] See *An Evidence Based History of Reiki*: http://www.spiritualone.com/Online/Oct13/OctNL13.htm#life. Also see p. 9 in this book.

[2] http://en.wikipedia.org/wiki/Shiken_haramitsu_daikoumyo.

As previously stated, the DKM is an accepted part of Western Usui Reiki, and it was assumed to have always been a part of the Usui System of Reiki Healing. However, recent information coming from Hiroshi Doi Sensei indicates that the Usui Reiki Ryoho Gakkai do not use the DKM symbol in their Reiki training. This information came to him in discussions he had with members of the Gakkai about the DKM, including those at the Shinpi-den (Master) level and several of the presidents of the Gakkai. In these conversations, they all indicated that they had never seen this symbol or Japanese concept used in conjunction with the practice of Reiki; according to their understanding, Usui Sensei did not use it.[4] Doi Sensei also indicates that the Gakkai use only three symbols which are given in the Okuden level; they are the same three that are taught in Reiki Level II in the Western/Takata style of Reiki. No additional symbol is given in the Gakkai Shinpi-den level.[5]

This information is corroborated by Arjava Petter, who was told by Fumio Ogawa Sensei, a Gakkai Shinpi-den member, that the DKM was not used by the Gakkai. He also asked Chiyoko Yamaguchi Sensei, who was a Shinpi-den through the Hayashi system, and she confirmed that Hayashi Sensei did not use this symbol either.[6]

We do know that Takata Sensei used this symbol. However, there is no clear evidence as to when she got it or from whom. Some say that it's possible that Takata Sensei may have gotten this symbol from Hayashi Sensei. But in considering this, we need to be aware of some of the details of the Reiki training of both Chiyoko Yamaguchi Sensei and Takata Sensei.

Takata Sensei received her Usui Reiki Master certificate from Hayashi Sensei in Honolulu, Hawaii in February 1938.[7] Chiyoko Yamaguchi Sensei took her first Reiki seminar from Hayashi Sensei in Ishikawa, Japan in March 1938. She was an avid student and helped Hayashi at his seminars whenever he came to teach in her town. Around 1940, with the permission of Hayashi

[3] Ingrid Fischer-Schreiber, Franz-Karl Ehrhard, Kurt Friedrichs, and Michael S. Diener, *The Encyclopedia of Eastern Philosophy and Religion* (Boston, MA: Shambhala, 1994).

[4] In an email from Doi Sensei he said there is misinformation being circulated about the Gakkai using the DKM which is most likely based on translation problems. He did meet one person who apparently studied with Usui Sensei who was shown the DKM as part of his training, not as a symbol, but as a spiritual concept, but this person was not a Gakkai member and no longer practices Reiki.

[5] William Lee Rand, "Interview With Hiroshi Doi Sensei, Part I" *Reiki News Magazine* (Spring 2014), p. 27.

[6] Frank Arjava Petter, *This is Reiki* (Twin Lakes, WI: Lotus Press, 2012), p. 174.

[7] Takata Sensei's Reiki Certificate in Marianne Streich, "How Hawayo Takata Practiced and Taught Reiki," *Reiki News Magazine*, Spring 1970, p. 17. See http://www.reiki.org/Download/TakataArticle.pdf.

Sensei, she was given the Shinpi-den level by her uncle, who was also a Shinpi-den.[8] At this time she was shown how to give reiju (attunements). Since Chiyoko Yamaguchi Sensei learned Shinpi-den after Takata Sensei and Chiyoko was able to give reiju or attunements and teach all the classes, it stands to reason that if Hayashi Sensei had added the DKM symbol to the system he taught, then it would have been taught to Chiyoko Yamaguchi Sensei. But as previously noted it was not, and it is her understanding that Hayashi Sensei did not use the DKM.

If Hayashi Sensei hadn't used the DKM symbol in his Reiki training, then how did Takata Sensei get it? Arjava Petter suggests that she may have gotten it from Iris Ishikuro.[9] Iris was one of the Master students of Takata Sensei and was also a friend.[10] She was also the first person who became a Reiki Master to received Reiki training from Takata Sensei, having received Reiki I in 1968. Iris Ishikuro had been a member of the Johrei Fellowship, which is a religion that practices hand healing. They use the DKM symbol as part of their spiritual training; therefore, it's possible that Iris introduced Takata Sensei to the DKM symbol. If this is true, then it's also possible that they collaborated to add the DKM to the attunement. Takata Sensei could also have decided to do this on her own after becoming aware of the symbol through Iris or from another source since it is a commonly known Japanese spiritual concept. And in fact, even though Hayashi Sensei didn't use the DKM symbol in his Reiki Training, it's still possible that she learned about the DKM from him. The idea that Takata Sensei added the DKM symbol to the practice of Reiki is not that difficult to assume. After all, we know that she had changed the system of Reiki she taught by eliminating the Japanese Reiki Techniques and creating her own system of hand placements called the "foundation treatment."[11] It would only be an additional step in this process to add a new symbol to the attunements she used. This may have been done to increase the effectiveness of Reiki and to further safeguard the Master training by introducing a symbol necessary to do attunements that is only available to those who took the training.

So from above mentioned research we see that Usui Sensei, the Usui Reiki Ryoho Gakkai and Hayashi Sensei did not use the DKM symbol. We also know

[8] Tadao Yamaguchi, *Light on the Origin of Reiki* (Twin Lakes, WI: Lotus Press, 2007), p. 35.

[9] Ibid., p. 174.

[10] Some stay Iris was Takata Sensei's cousin, but according to her daughter, they were not related.

[11] John Harvey Gray and Lourdes Gray, *Hand to Hand, The Longest Practicing Reiki Master Tells His Story* (Bloomington, IN: Ixlibris, 2002), p. 93.

that Takata Sensei did use it. So while the evidence is circumstantial, it appears that Takata Sensei is most likely the one who added the DKM symbol to the practice of Usui Reiki.

So the question at this point is should we continue to use the DKM if it wasn't part of Usui or Hayashi Reiki? When we look at the evidence based history of Reiki it is clear that both Usui Sensei and Hayashi Sensei made developmental changes to the practice of Usui Reiki.[12] Therefore, it appears to be a practice that is not meant to remain static, but a practice that is meant to evolve.

The DKM symbol has been in use for over 40 years, and it is used by the vast majority of Reiki Masters. My experience and that of all those I've talked to about it is that the DKM is a powerful symbol that makes the practice of Reiki more effective. Therefore, the DKM symbol can be thought of as a positive contribution and an important part of the continued development of Usui Reiki.

Because of this, it is appropriate that we express gratitude toward Takata Sensei for her addition of the DKM symbol to the practice of Usui Reiki and be thankful for the improvements it has made to the practice of Reiki and the increased benefit it has brought to all those in need of healing. With the understanding that Usui Reiki was meant to be developed, we can only wonder about the improvements that are in store for us as we continue to grow as healers and follow the guidance Reiki provides.

[12] William Lee Rand, "An Interview with Hiroshi Doi," *Reiki News Magazine*, Pts. 1 and 2 (Summer 2003): p. 9–11; (Fall 2003): p. 12–14. http://www.reikimembership.com/articlesforms/hiroshidoiinterview.pdf. Also see p. 69 and 75 in this book.

How Hawayo Takata Practiced and Taught Reiki

BY MARIANNE STREICH

ALL WESTERN Reiki practitioners have a lineage going back through Mrs. Takata. It was she who brought Reiki to the West. Without her, it is unlikely that anyone outside Japan would even recognize the word "Reiki" today, much less know the wonderful gift of its healing power.

Takata practiced and taught Reiki for more than forty years. She was a powerful healer, an engaging teacher, and a successful businesswoman. She facilitated amazing healings, attuned countless men, women, and children to Reiki, and managed a number of business enterprises. What she did not do was leave comprehensive records about her work.

Unlike Usui sensei and Hayashi sensei, Takata did not provide her students with a manual or printed materials.[1]

Mrs. Takata at the Baylow home, June 11, 1979. (Photo taken by G. Baylow.)

[1] Dr. Hayashi's manual is translated and reprinted in *Reiki, The Healing Touch, First and Second Degree Manual* by William Lee Rand (Michigan: Vision Publications, 2000). A partial translation of Dr. Usui's manual is available in *The Original Reiki Handbook of Dr. Mikao Usui: The Traditional Usui Reiki Ryoho Treatment Positions and Numerous Reiki Techniques for Health and Well-Being* by Mikao Usui, Frank Arjava Petter (Wisconsin: Lotus Press, 2000).

She did not allow the taking of notes during her classes; her teaching was in the oral tradition, and she expected her students to store her words in memory. Likewise, papers on which students practiced drawing the Reiki symbols were destroyed at the end of each class.[2] Takata had no prepared text and so each of her classes was somewhat different.[3] She left no known written records of her work or philosophy.

In part because of her oral system of teaching, many rumors and myths have developed about her over the years, and it can be challenging to reconstruct accurate information. We must rely on the memories and writings of the twenty-two Masters (see list page 98) she trained and on her Level I and II students to reconstruct her methods of practicing and teaching. This I have attempted to do, accessing as many sources and materials as possible.

The sign for Takata's office was discovered in the basement of her clinic by Reiki Master Duff Cady in 1995. The clinic was located at 2070 Kilauea Ave. in Hilo, Hawaii. The word "Reiki" is visible behind the lettering. The change from Reiki to "Short Wave Treatments" was probably in response to anti-Japanese sentiment after the bombing of Pearl Harbor in December of 1941. The building currently houses the Kline Chiropractic Clinic. Dr. Kline, an Aikido instructor and healer, has set up a small shrine on the upper floor to honor Hawayo Takata.

Takata's Training

In her book, *Living Reiki*,[4] Fran Brown describes Takata's training as Takata explained it to her. According to Brown, Takata spent a year of internship at Dr. Hayashi's clinic in Tokyo, beginning in 1935. She was initiated into the First Degree of Reiki over four days. On the first day, students were taught basic hand positions

[2] Amy Z. Rowland, in "A Tribute to Traditional Reiki Master, Rev. Beth Gray," *Reiki News Magazine* (Spring 2003), p. 10, states: "She [Beth Gray, one of the twenty-two Masters that Takata trained] had promised Takata that she would collect all drawings of the symbols at the close of each Level II class, and afterwards, burn them. And this she did."

[3] Dr. Paul V. Johnson, president Spiritual Advisory Council, in a letter to William Lee Rand dated April 19, 1994 states: "I sat in on a number [of her classes] and all were somewhat different as she had no prepared text." (Johnson was a Level I and II student of Takata's. He and his wife hosted Takata in their home for several of these classes during 1975-1976.)

4 Fran Brown, *Living Reiki, Takata's Teachings* (California: LifeRhythm, 1992), p. 29-30.

for treating above the neck and the conditions and diseases common to those areas. On day two, they were taught hand positions and treatment of conditions of the front of the body and on day three, the back. Day four was devoted to treatment of acute cases and accidents and to discussion of the spiritual aspects of Reiki and the Five Ideals. Each student was given a copy of Hayashi's healing guide, which gave a list of diseases and the hand positions that were to be used in the treatment of each condition. He also emphasized that there is always a cause and an effect; eliminate the cause and there will be no effect.

Massage

Reiki treatments, massage, cabinet baths. Mrs. H. Takata, 2070 Kilauea Ave., Waiakea Homesteads.

This is an ad for Takata's Hilo practice, which appeared in the local *Tribune Herald*, March 3, 1941, prior to the attack on Pearl Harbor.

Mrs. Takata by Ursula Baylow's garden near Skaha Lake, Penticton, BC, June, 1979. (Photo taken by G. Baylow.)

After this training, Hayashi's students spent mornings in his clinic working in pairs to treat patients and afternoons making house calls, giving treatments that typically lasted an hour to an hour and a half each. At the end of her year of internship, she was given an examination and allowed to progress to the Second Degree or *Oku Den*.[5] After this more training was offered. A May 1936 entry in Takata's diary reads:

> What was more than pleasing was that Mr. Hayashi has granted to bestow upon me the secret of *Shinpe Den*, *Kokiyu-ho* and the *Leiji-ho* the utmost secret in the Energy Science. Know [sic] one can imagine my happiness to think that I have the honor and respect to be trusted with this gift a gift of a life time and I promised within me to do my utmost in regard to this beautiful and wonderful teaching that I just received—I fully promise

[5] I have found no information regarding the content of her Oku Den, or Second Degree training with Dr. Hayashi.

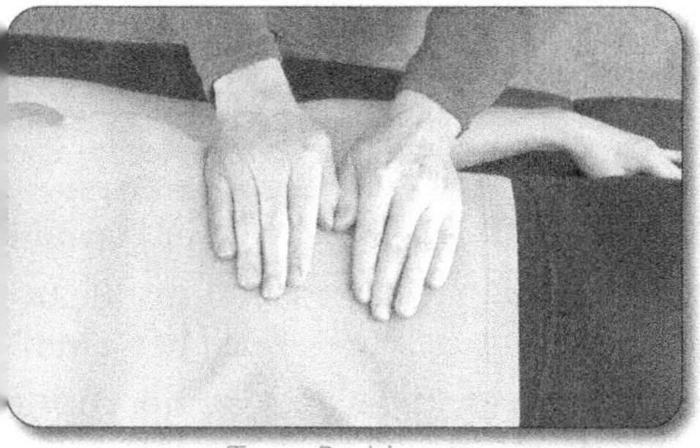
Torso Position 1

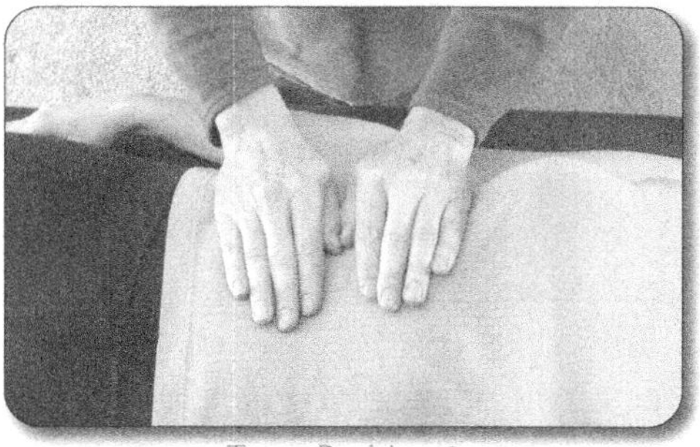
Torso Position 2

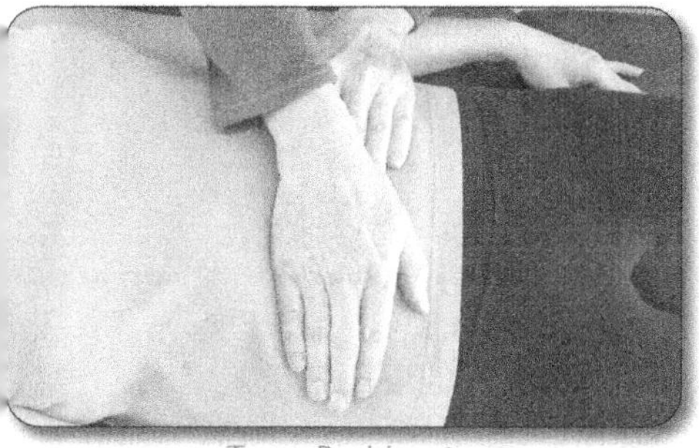
Torso Position 3

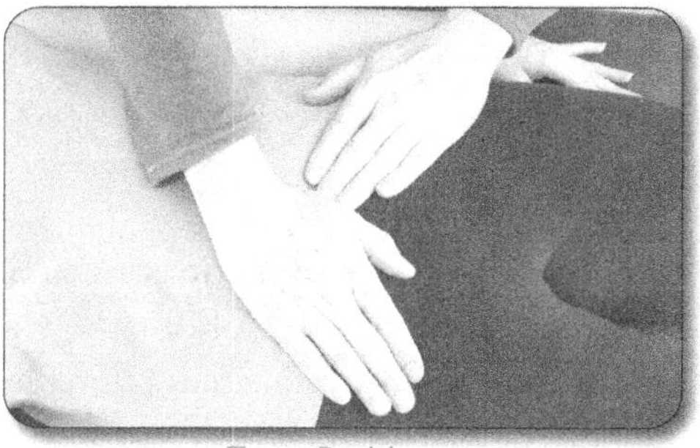
Torso Position 4

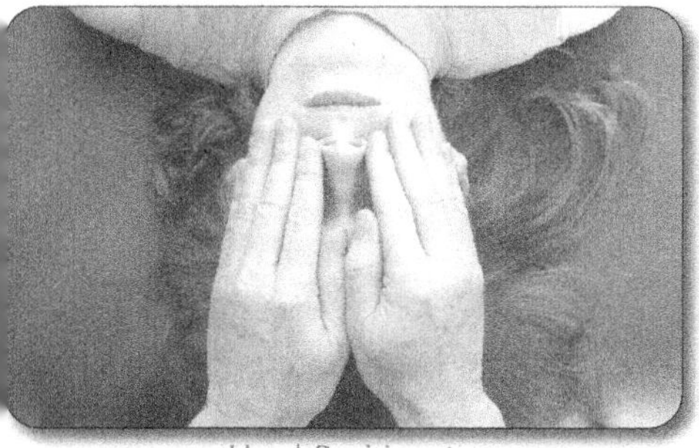
Head Position 1

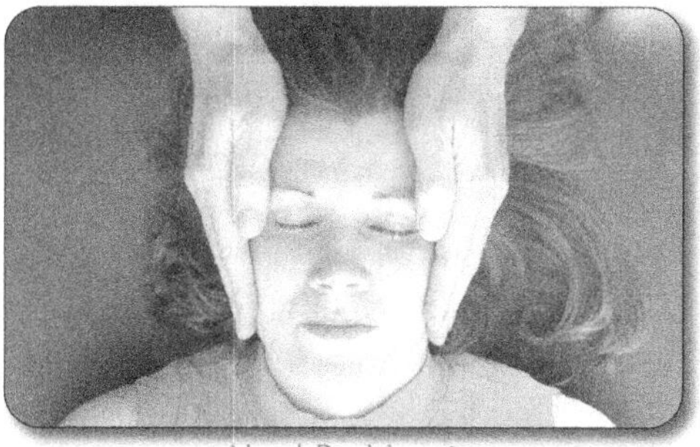
Head Position 2

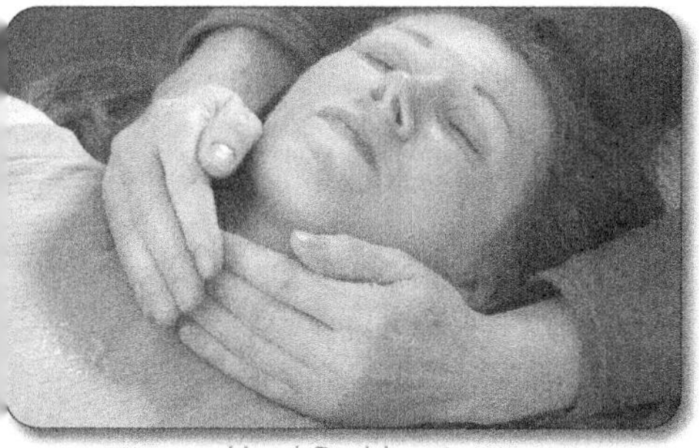
Head Position 3

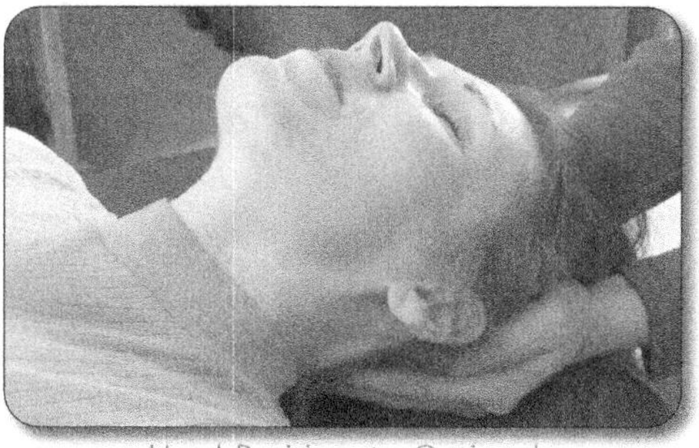
Head Position 4 - Optional

to do what is right thru sincereness [sic] and to do my utmost in kindness and shall regard and respect the teaching and it's teacher with utmost reverence and respect.[6]

In the summer of 1937[7] Takata returned to Kauai. A few weeks later Hayashi sensei came to visit her. He stayed for six months, giving classes and treatments with Takata briefly on Kauai, then in Honolulu. Hayashi sensei issued her a Master certificate on February 21, 1938 (see photo page 100). To avoid licensing issues, the following year Takata studied at the National College of Drugless Physicians in Chicago and also received a license to practice massage in Honolulu. (Brown, 68) In October of 1939 she moved her office to Hilo on the big island where she remained for the next ten years. (Brown, 71)

Takata's Practice

Takata's Reiki treatment consisted of what she called a "foundation treatment" followed by a search for the cause of the condition and additional Reiki applied in those specific areas related to the cause. She advocated repeated treatments, daily if possible, for chronic conditions. And she welcomed what she called "healing reactions" as a sign that the body was beginning to heal itself.

According to Takata-trained Master John Harvey Gray,[8] Takata combined many of the hand positions taught by Dr. Hayashi to create her "foundation treatment," which she used as a standard procedure for each client. In contrast, Hayashi employed a specific combination of positions to treat specific conditions. In his clinic, two practitioners worked together to give a treatment, whereas Takata worked alone, giving treatments sitting on the floor in a cross-legged fashion. (Gray, 97)

Her foundation treatment focused on the torso and the head. According to Gray, there were four basic hand positions for the torso and three for the head.

[6] Hawayo Takata, unpublished diary. Shinpe Den is the master level, Kokiyu-ho is the dry bathing technique and Leiji-ho is the intuitive method of finding where to place one's hands.

[7] Helen Joyce Haberly, *Reiki: Hawayo Takata's Story* (Maryland: Archedigm Publications, 2000 Memorial Edition), p. 33. Fran Brown gives 1936 as the year of Takata's return to Kauai; however, since Haberly's text was authorized by Takata and much of it was written during Takata's lifetime, 1937 seems the more likely date. In addition, the date of Takata's Master certificate also supports the later date.

[8] John Harvey Gray and Lourdes Gray with Steven McFadden and Elisabeth Clark, *Hand to Hand, The Longest-Practicing Reiki Master Tells His Story* (Gray, 2002).

Summer 1979, at Penticton BC, with Ursula Baylow, when she completed her training as Reiki Master. (photo taken by G. Baylow)

(Gray, 93). There were none over the heart or on the back, although she added optional positions over the heart, the back, and on the back of the head, depending on the nature of the client's problem. The first hand position in a foundation treatment covered the area of the stomach, pancreas, and spleen.[9] The second position covered the liver and gall bladder, a third covered the transverse colon and the small intestine, and the fourth placement covered the reproductive system, ascending and descending colon, and bladder (see photos page 89). Brown reports that Takata admonished her students to spend half of the treatment time on the front torso, as it is the "main factory" of the body, processing the fuel that the body takes in (Brown 29).

After treating the torso, Takata then moved to the head, using three positions, and sometimes adding a fourth on the back of the head. The first position covered the eyes; with the second, hands were placed on either side of the head, and in the third, hands were placed on the neck. This was a complete foundation treatment. On many occasions, according to Gray, Takata remarked that she had simplified the system (Gray, 94).

Gray reports that Takata's foundation treatment began with the torso (Gray, 93), although other practitioners recall her starting with the head. Helen Haberly reports that Takata sometimes started a treatment with the head, at other times with the abdomen. At times she told her students that it didn't matter as long as the complete treatment was given. (Haberly, 50) In some instances she indicated that the nature of the condition determines where the treatment should start. "The complete treatment is given, but in these cases [arthritis and rheumatism] we start with the abdomen." (Haberly, 73) And again, "For all types, [of cancer]

[9] Although Gray indicates on page 93 that the first position is over the liver, a later reference on page 98 and photo on page 115 make it clear that the first position is over the stomach, pancreas and spleen. Haberly's text also indicates that the first position is over the stomach.

the same procedure is used: the complete treatment is given. Start from the head, then treat all of the glands on the front of the body. Turn the patient over and complete the back. Last of all, go to the affected area." (Haberly, 99)

One of Takata's guiding principles, which she emphasized repeatedly, was to treat both cause and effect. "If you treat only the afflicted area of the body, you may alleviate symptoms temporarily but permanent healing will not take place unless you treat the cause." (Gray, 80) Takata's training and experience had taught her that the cause of a condition is often centered, not in the affected area of the body, but elsewhere. She tells of treating a young woman who had become blind around the age of thirteen for no apparent reason. She was brought to Takata three years later after attempts to discover the cause of her condition through traditional medicine had failed. Had Takata only treated the girl's eyes, she would not have discovered that the cause of the condition was actually in the ovaries. Takata treated her daily for 28 days, giving a full treatment and additional energy to the ovaries and eyes. On the 28th day, she could see again. (Gray, 81)

To locate the cause, Takata used her intuition. This was likely a simplified version of *Leiji-ho* (also called *Reiji-ho*), a technique taught to her by Hayashi.[10] She also used the sensitivity in her hands to locate the cause by noticing a stronger or different vibration when her hands were over the part of the body where the cause of a condition was centered. This was probably a simplified version of Byosen scanning. She told her students, "Reiki will guide you. Let the Reiki hands find it. They will know what to do." (Haberly, 58)

At times Takata started a treatment in the area where the cause was located. Haberly relates that a man came to Takata with the complaint that he suffered headaches every evening. Takata began treating his abdomen in the area of his gall bladder. When he protested that he had a headache, not a stomachache, she explained that she felt "much vibration in my hands" when she reached the area of his gall bladder and felt that the cause of his discomfort was there. She followed this by working on his head and his back, giving a full treatment. The client reported that by the time she came to his head, the pain was gone. (Haberly, 78) For breast cancer or any condition involving the breasts, Takata advocated special emphasis on the ovaries, uterus (torso position 4) and thyroid, (head position 3) as she found that the cause of the condition was often located in these areas. (Haberly, 99-100)

"Takata always encouraged complete and frequent Reiki treatments for long-lasting chronic problems, daily, if possible. She emphasized that if a health problem or

[10] Takata's diary, unpublished.

illness has been around for three weeks or more, the whole body is involved in the healing process and therefore a full treatment is indicated." (Gray, 81) In the recounting of her stories, Takata frequently mentions giving treatments daily, sometimes several times a day, over lengthy periods of time. In a case of shingles, for instance, she reports giving the client treatment daily for two months, by which time the pain had disappeared. The client took Reiki and continued to treat herself daily afterwards. (Haberly, 95) In another case, Takata treated a young woman with epilepsy. "We began treatments in October and by the Spring I said she did not have to come to me any more, for the family could treat her at home. She continued to improve, and in this way she was entirely cured of epilepsy." (Haberly, 69-70)

Haberly quotes Takata as saying, "Except for shock or accident, use the full treatment, and this is the same for all things. Don't try to take only the parts. The body is a complete unit, so whenever possible, treat it completely. Start with the abdomen or the head—it doesn't matter—then proceed with the whole treatment. It is the same for all, whether physical or mental. There is no difference in the treatment." (Haberly, 59)

When treating someone who had experienced trauma, Takata would "release shock from the adrenal glands" by placing the hands over the adrenal glands and giving Reiki until the flow of energy diminished. Gray quotes Takata as saying, "There will not be complete healing after an injury if you don't release the shock from the adrenals." (Gray, 172)

At the end of a treatment, Takata used a technique that involved running the fingers on either side of the spine and manipulating tissue from the neck to coccyx to improve blood circulation. (Gray, 94) (This technique is sometimes referred to as "The Reiki Finish" or "Nerve Stroke.") Since performing this technique requires a massage license in many jurisdictions, Gray and other practitioners have devised alternate techniques that accomplish the same goal without manipulation of tissue. One method is to sweep the hands through the energy field from head to foot several times.

To ensure that her clients received treatment on a regular basis, Takata often attuned members of their families, and in at least one instance, their neighbors. Helen Haberly relates a story about a young woman who had advanced tuberculosis. Takata gave her treatments every day for a week and then gave classes to her mother and their neighbors so that she could have many people treating her. According to Takata, she completely recovered within six months. (Haberly, 82)

After a treatment, especially one for a chronic condition, Takata expected the client to experience a "healing reaction." This was a release of toxins by the body and could take the form of gastrointestinal upset, flu-like symptoms, headache, or in some instances an intensification of the condition itself. (Haberly, 69) Takata welcomed healing reactions because "the reaction shows whether the healing is moving forward." (Brown, 92) According to Haberly, Takata taught that chronic conditions requiring long-term treatment are more likely to be accompanied by reactions that release toxins. If injuries are quickly treated they are not as likely to produce reactions. (Haberly, 55)

Although most of Takata's stories focus on the treatment of illness, she also emphasized the importance of Reiki to ensure health and well-being. For instance, regarding Reiki and pregnancy, she is quoted as saying, "The best plan is to start Reiki before becoming pregnant, and then have treatments to strengthen her during the pregnancy; and if any symptoms then appear, Reiki could be applied immediately." (Haberly, 67)

Whatever the condition, Takata's philosophy was to "give a good treatment and release it to God. Leave it to God how healing will come about." (Brown, 95)

How Takata Taught

Takata taught in Hawaii for a number of years before starting to teach classes on the mainland in the 1970's. The first mainland class she taught that included students of non-Japanese origin was taught on Orcas Island off the coast of Washington state in 1973. (Gray, 71) She often held classes in private homes, teaching a number of classes from 1974-1977 in Redmond, CA at the home of Beth and John Harvey Gray. Before her death in 1980, she had traveled the world teaching countless students and training twenty-two Masters.

Takata's Reiki I classes were typically taught over the course of three or four evenings in sessions that typically lasted two hours but could, at times, go on for up to four hours, according to Brown. (Brown, 94) She did not work from a prepared text, so the content, as well as the length of the classes, varied. She began with an explanation of Universal energy, "Here is the great space which surrounds us—the Universe. There is endless and enormous energy. It is universal…its ultimate source is the Creator…it can stem from the sun, or moon or stars…. It is a limitless force. It is the source of energy that makes the plants grow…the birds fly. When a human being has pain, problems, he or she can draw from it. It is an ethereal source, a wave length of great power which can revitalize, restore harmony."[11]

[11] Fran Brown, "Mrs. Takata Opens Minds to Reiki," San Mateo, *The Times*, May 17, 1975.

She told the story of Usui sensei in installments over the course of the class, a segment prior to each of four attunements. She demonstrated and explained hand positions. She was very precise about the placement of the hands. Master Wanja Twan remembers "Mrs. Takata's crisp teachings and precise hand positions, a perfect technician…"[12] A student of Master Beth Gray reports that Beth Gray's students were taught to keep their hands in the same position through an entire cycle of energy [until the practitioner begins to feel energy ebb in the hands] and were told that was Takata's teaching.[13]

During her classes, Takata told numerous stories about her forty-plus years of experience with the treatment of various conditions from tuberculosis to blindness to arthritis to headache. A natural storyteller with a keen sense of humor, her tales were entertaining as well as instructive. She talked about the Five Reiki Ideals. She used repetition to make sure that each of her students understood, as she did not allow the taking of notes or taping of classes.[14] (She did allow John Gray to tape some of the stories she told during her classes, and one of those tapes is available.)[15]

Classes were focused and intense. Anneli Twan (daughter of Master Wanja Twan) remembers Takata as "an exceedingly efficient teacher….when that little Japanese fireball said 'jump' everyone jumped."[16] Robert Shingledecker, a student who hosted Takata's classes in his home, recalls, "Mrs. Takata took her Reiki very seriously and could be a taskmaster and disciplinarian, but she was also sweet, even motherly to us and had a heart bigger than she was."[17]

[12] Wanja Twan, Web posting, www.morningstarproductions.ca/page2.htm

[13] Amy Z. Rowland, "A Tribute to Traditional Reiki Master, Rev. Beth Gray" *Reiki News Magazine* (Spring 2003), p. 10.

[14] The information in this paragraph is cited in numerous sources, including, John Harvey Gray, Fran Brown, Amy Z. Rowland (student of Beth Gray), Sarah Baylow, daughter of Ursula Baylow, Anneli Twan, daughter of Wanja Twan, and others who took Level I and II from Takata.

[15] "Takata Speaks, Volume I Reiki Stories," Selections and Introductions by John Harvey Gray, available through Gray's Website: www.mv.com/ipusers/reiki/

[16] Anneli Twan, from a talk quoted on Holistic Vancouver Website: http://www.holisticvancouver.com/news/article.php?story_id=125. Twan received her first attunement in the spring of 1979 at the age of ten. She received her Master level from her mother, Wanja Twan with the help of Phyllis Furumoto (Takata's granddaughter) and taught her first class at the age of sixteen.

[17] William R. Shingledecker, 1997 Web posting: www.create.org/healingarts/takata.htm. This site is no longer active.

Reiki Juice

Takata recommended a diet of vegetables, fruits, whole grains, fish and chicken. She also had a home remedy, a drink which she drank and recommended to her clients and students. (Some of her students called it the Takata Cocktail.) She said it purifies the blood and energizes the whole body. Helen Haberly mentions it in, *Reiki: Hawayo Takata's Story*, but does not give an actual recipe. Being a juicer, I was curious and experimented with the ingredients. Here's what I came up with:

All ingredients should be organic, but if not, then make sure you wash them with a vegetable wash to remove pesticidial residues and chemical sprays (available in most health food stores).

1	beet about 2 inches in diameter. You can also include some of the greens.
1	tablespoon watercress or about 10 small leaves.
2	stalks of celery
1	medium carrot
2	cups purified or spring water.
3-5	minutes Reiki

Chop up all ingredients and place in a high speed blender such as a Vita Mix. Before blending, place your hands on the blender container and give Reiki to the ingredients for several minutes. Start the blender and continue giving Reiki until the mixture is liquefied.

In addition to being a blood purifier, this concoction is a powerful detoxifier, especially for the liver, gallbladder and lungs. The affects of this drink are very beneficial, but caution should be exercised when first starting to consume it because it is such a powerful detoxifier.

Drink only about half the juice at first, placing the remainder in the refrigerator. Wait an hour or more before drinking more to discover how your body will respond to it. Once you've determined the amount that is right for you, it's important that you drink Reiki Juice every day as its beneficial effects take place over time. It has a really fresh wholesome flavor but a little on the tart side. Drinking it gives you increased mental clarity, a feeling of lightness, energy and vitality that will only increase as your body detoxifies.

—William Lee Rand

Shingledecker remembers that she talked about different illnesses and how to treat them and emphasized certain "no no's" such as "never lay hands on the spine—always come in from an angle[18] and never remove your hands from the patient—even when rolling him/her over."[19] He relates that Takata told him privately that a Reiki practitioner should remove all jewelry prior to giving a Reiki session because it can get very hot. (Shingledecker, Web posting)

Takata advocated to her students and clients a diet of vegetables, fruits, whole grains, fish and chicken. Helen Haberly mentions a recipe for a Reiki Juice home remedy that Takata concocted, which consisted of watercress, beets, carrots, and celery blended together. Takata claimed that it was a blood builder that energized the entire body. (Haberly, 48) Shingledecker refers to this as the "Takata Cocktail," of which he said, "...it looked gorgeous...but tasted horrible!" He recalled that it had a number of ingredients, including beet greens, and said that Takata insisted that he drink it every day when she was holding classes in his home. (Shingledecker, Web posting) An avid juicer, William Rand has experimented with the ingredients and devised a recipe (See page 96).

Takata stressed to her students the importance of treating themselves. " 'You are Number One!' she would say, 'Then if you have time, treat your family and your friends; but in Reiki Healing, you first, then other people.' " (Haberly, 56) After the Level I attunement, Takata had her students give her treatments each evening.[20] "She told us that when one practices Reiki they would have health, happiness, security and should prepare for a long life... she once told me that when you had pure Reiki flowing through you, you could not make a bad decision." (Shingledecker, Web posting)

There is less information available as to how Takata taught her Level II or "Distant Healing" classes as they were called. She taught the three symbols and how to give distant Reiki. Initially, only the dominant hand was initiated during the Level II attunement.[21] This was later changed either by Takata or some of her Masters. It is now common practice to initiate both hands.

[18] Not touching the spine may have come from the idea that only a licensed chiropractor should touch the spine, but we know from experience that the spine can be treated without harm as long as one doesn't manipulate the vertebra.

[19] John Gray, in a telephone conversation January 30, 2007 told the author that, to his knowledge, Takata never suggested a practitioner should keep his/her hands on the client throughout the treatment.

[20] Dr. Paul V. Johnson, letter to William Rand, April 19, 1994.

[21] Rowland mentions this, as do other practitioners.

Takata's Masters

	First	Second	Master
Iris Ishikuro	1967		?
Kay Yamashita			before 1976
John Harvey Gray	06/1974		10/6/1976
Virginia W. Samdahl		1975	before 10/1976
Ethel Lombardi	1976?	1976?	1976
Dorothy Baba			1977
Barbara Lincoln McCullough		1977	
Harry M. Kuboi			04/1977
Fran Brown	06/1973	1977	01/15/1979
Phyllis Lei Furumoto			04/1979
Ursula Baylow	07/ 7/1976	08/25/1978	06/11/1979
Barbara Weber	08/1978	10/1978	09/1979
Barbara Brown			10/1979
Beth Gray	1973		10/1979
Bethal Phaigh	Spring 1979	10/1979	10/1979
Wanja Twan	Summer 1978	Spring 1979	10/1979
George Araki			11/1979
Paul Mitchell			11/1979
Shinobu Saito		1978	05/1980
Mary McFadyen			09/1980
Patricia Bowling			09/1980
Rick Bockner	10/10/1979	10/20/1979	10/12/1980

In some instances, Takata gave two attunements during the Level II class rather than one. According to Rowland, "The attunement process using two attunements... opened up a special channel in the mind of the practitioner which facilitated an intuitive ability. This enhanced the practitioner's ability to communicate with the subconscious mind of the client to find the original cause of an illness or condition and also allowed the practitioner to communicate with the clients Higher Self."[22] This information was accessed through the use of the Mental/Emotional symbol, which Beth Gray also called "the talking symbol." (Rowland, 10) When two attunements are given, the second is a repeat of the

[22] In the same article, Rowland states: "As far as I know, Takata taught only three other Reiki Masters she initiated to use the second symbol in an intuitive way, and she did not teach them identically..."

first according to John Gray. In his experience, whether the second attunement increases a student's intuition varies depending on the student.[23]

Little mention is made of the length of the Level II classes or the specifics of what was taught, except for the learning of symbols. Several sources relate that Takata sometimes taught Level II back to back with Level I,[24] although a time period for Level II is not mentioned. She was very exacting about the teaching of the symbols and had students practice them over and over. After the class, she burned all of the practice papers, as students were to have memorized them. Takata considered the symbols sacred and admonished her students that they were not to be shown to anyone who was not already attuned to Reiki.[25]

Paul Johnson hosted classes in his Golf, Illinois home in 1975-1976. He states that the class in which he and his wife and eight others were initiated into Reiki II in 1976 lasted only two hours, with Takata commenting that the group was "exceptionally gifted" and caught on quickly. The class consisted largely of learning to draw the three symbols.[26]

Master Wanja Twan reports that she took part in five Level I classes and three Level II classes taught by Takata in rural British Columbia in the late 70's, one of which was a special class for children.[27] Twan took Level I in summer 1978, Level II in spring of 1979 and Master in October of 1979. At the time she received Master, a class was held in which she assisted, "...there were so many people gathered, Mrs. Takata at this time instructed me as if she was an army sergeant how to do the actual teachings [Level I] and the mechanics of it. Ten people indicated that they wanted their second degree at that time, so I had good practice in that as well."[28]

[22] In the same article, Rowland states: "As far as I know, Takata taught only three other Reiki Masters she initiated to use the second symbol in an intuitive way, and she did not teach them identically..."

[23] John Gray, telephone conversation with the author, January 30, 2007.

[24] Wanja Twan, Paul Johnson, and Shingledecker in Web postings and letter previously cited.

[25] It is safe to say that virtually all of her students and Masters would agree on this.

[26] Paul V. Johnson in a letter to William Rand dated March 14, 1994.

[27] Wanja Twan's ten-year-old daughter, Anneli was initiated by Takata to Level I at the same time that Wanja received Level II. Anneli took her own children to Hawaii to be initiated at an early age, although Takata was no longer living. Takata believed, according to a statement by Anneli Twan in a talk given at a Vancouver Area Reiki Masters Gathering, that the best age to initiate children is between four and five. (See footnote #15.) Sarah Baylow reports in an email to Rand dated October 22, 2006 that her mother, Master Ursula Baylow, initiated Sarah's son and nephew before they were nine years old.

[28] Wanja Twan, Web posting, www.morningstarproductions.ca/page2.htm

CERTIFICATE

THIS IS TO CERTIFY that Mrs. Hawayo Takata, an American citizen born in the Territory of Hawaii, after a course of study and training in the Usui system of Reiki healing undertaken under my personal supervision during a visit to Japan in 1935 and subsequently, has passed all the tests and proved worthy and capable of administering the treatment and of conferring the power of Reiki on others.

THEREFORE I, Dr. Chujiro Hayashi, by virtue of my authority as a Master of the Usui Reiki system of drugless healing, do hereby confer upon Mrs. Hawayo Takata the full power and authority to practice the Reiki system and to impart to others the secret knowledge and the gift of healing under this system.

MRS. HAWAYO TAKATA is hereby certified by me as a practitioner and Master of Dr. Usui's Reiki system of healing, at this time the only person in the United States authorized to confer similar powers on others and one of the thirteen fully qualified as a Master of the profession.

Signed by me this 21st day of February, 1938, in the city and county of Honolulu, territory of Hawaii.

(SIGNED) Chujiro Hayashi

Witness to his signature:
Yoshio Hanao

TERRITORY OF HAWAII, }
City and County of Honolulu. } ss.

On this 21st day of February A. D. 1938 before me personally appeared
* * * * * * * * * * * * *(DR.) CHUJIRO HAYASHI* * * * * * * * * * * * * * * * * *
to me known to be the person described in and who executed the foregoing instrument and acknowledged that WHO executed the same as HIS free act and deed.

W. Silva
Notary Public, First Judicial Circuit,
Territory of Hawaii.

Length of time period between Level II and Master Level and the length of the Master Level training itself also varied. Fran Brown relates that she took Level I from Takata in 1973, Level II in 1977 and was initiated as Takata's seventh Master in January 1979.[29] Although she doesn't specify the number of sessions nor the total hours of training, she states in her book, *Living Reiki*, that she and Takata were snowbound for a week during her Master training and that she team taught with Takata as part of her training. (Brown, 94)

Bethal Phaigh's experience was quite different. She received Level II and Master initiations within a few days of each other. "Now I have to drive two hundred miles back to the Slocan [British Columbia] to get the money [for the Master training] and then back again to Lumby, [to] be initiated as a Master. All this and second degree within a few days!"[30] She continues, "I had left Hawaii that spring [1979] not knowing of Reiki. I return this winter as a Reiki Master, a very green one." (Phaigh, 132) That same winter she met up with Takata again on the Big Island, where Takata was visiting for one day only. That evening Takata reattuned Phaigh. (Phaigh, 133)

In addition to Brown, some of the other Masters Takata trained, including Virginia Samdahl and Phyllis Furomoto, may have traveled with her as part of their training, but this seems not to have been the case for most of them.[31] John Gray has no memory of any of the other Masters serving such an apprenticeship.[32]

In her Master classes, Takata taught four attunements for Level I and one or perhaps two for Level II.[33] She gave one Master symbol. The focus of the Master training was on learning how to pass attunements. Twan quotes Takata as instructing her Master students, "Keep it [instruction] simple or people will forget." (Twan, Web posting)

Her Legacy

Mrs. Takata made her transition on December 25, 1980, just short of her eightieth birthday. Without her, it is very unlikely that Reiki would ever have

29 Fran Brown, Web posting, www.reikifranbrown.com/bio.htm.

30 Bethal Phaigh, *Journey Into Consciousness* (unpublished manuscript), p. 130.

31 Robert Frueston, a student of Fran Brown's, in a Web posting, www.robertfueston.com and Johnson in an April 19, 1994 letter to Rand.

32 John Gray, telephone conversation with the author, January 30, 2007.

33 John Gray asserts that Takata taught only one attunement for Level II and that he added the second attunement method. See footnote #21 for Amy Rowland's perspective.

reached the West. Certainly there was little communication and cultural interaction between Japan and the West in the late 1930's when she learned Reiki and brought it to Hawaii, and it is highly unlikely that Japanese practitioners would have had any thought or desire of exporting Reiki to the West in the aftermath of World War II.

The impact that Reiki has had in the world is largely due to Takata's extraordinary talents as a healer and teacher, the considerable force of her personality, and her astute business sense. It is impossible to count the number of students she taught, or to assess the impact of her teachings on countless lives or to measure the power of the tide that carries the gift of Reiki forward. Those of us who practice, teach, and live Reiki cannot but pay homage to this remarkable woman.

Origin of Usui Shiki Ryoho

BY WILLIAM LEE RAND

TAKATA SENSEI CALLED the style of Reiki she taught Usui Shiki Ryoho. This term appeared on the certificates she gave her students. However, as of June, 2015, I have been unable to discover where this term originated. According to Doi Sensei, this term was not used in Japan; neither Usui Sensei nor Hayashi Sensei used it and the Usui Reiki Ryoho Gakkai have no information about it. Doi Sensei says his understanding is that it came from the West. If this is true, then it's possible that Takata Sensei was the first to use it. This would not be that unlikely because as described on page 29, the style of Reiki she taught was unique being considerably different from what had been taught by Usui Sensei and Hayashi Sensei.[1] However, at this point, we don't if Takata originated it as definitive information about its origin has not been discovered.

[1] Some of the differences include the fact that Usui and Hayashi had just one attunement they did over and over and encouraged their students to receive as many as possible while Takata had a different attunement for each level and gave only one attunement or one set of attunements for each level and discouraged students from receiving more attunements. Also, Takata used a Master symbol whereas Usui and Hayashi did not use a Master symbol.

Takata's Handouts

BY WILLIAM LEE RAND

AFTER RECEIVING HER TRAINING from Hayashi Sensei during a year-long internship at his clinic in Japan, Mrs. Takata brought Reiki to Hawaii in 1938. She became an accomplished healer, practicing and teaching Reiki until her passing in 1980, a period of over 40 years. This was a great accomplishment, as her work prevented Reiki from falling into obscurity after World War II, and allowed Reiki to become established as a popular practice. It has since grown to include millions of practitioners worldwide.

After World War II, circumstances in Japan greatly curtailed the availability of information about Reiki. Takata became the main source. Takata changed the system of Reiki from what she was taught by Hayashi Sensei. According to John Harvey Gray, one of her Master students, Takata told him she had simplified the system, making it easier for Westerners to learn.[1] This included eliminating the hand position system she had been taught and replacing it with seven or eight positions, which she called the foundation treatment. She also left out many of the important healing techniques she had learned from Hayashi Sensei.

Even though she had changed Hayashi's system, the dominant idea she promoted to most of her students was that she was teaching the unaltered system created by Usui Sensei. There were also factual errors in her version of Reiki history. Not having any other source of information about Reiki, students were inclined to believe her. This idea continued to be promoted by some of her students after her passing, thus perpetuating misinformation and discouraging research into how Reiki had been practiced by its founders.

Fortunately, curiosity prevailed and in the 1990's several researchers including Toshitaka Mochizuki, Frank Arjava Petter and Hiroshi Doi began providing professionally researched and verifiable information about how Hayashi and Usui had practiced Reiki. This information included the location of Usui Sensei's grave and memorial stone, and contact with the Usui Reiki Ryoho Gakkai in Japan. We now have a much clearer picture of the history and practice of Reiki. Today, most of the original methods are being taught by various Reiki schools.

Despite the myths she created, it's important to remember that Takata was an excellent healer and that she accumulated invaluable experience over her 40 years of

[1] John Harvey Gray and Lourdes Gray with Steven McFadden and Elisabeth Clark, *Hand to Hand: The Longest-Practicing Reiki Master Tells His Story* (Gray 2002), p. 93.

practice. In addition, the system she created, though different than what she had been taught, is an effective healing system. It's important that we have a clear idea of how she practiced for historical reasons, but it also has value because of the usefulness of her healing and teaching methods. Therefore, it's important that we forgive her for the confusion some of her methods created and honor her for the value of her legacy.

One of the myths that Takata created is that Reiki is an oral tradition. Although she herself had been given a manual by Hayashi,[2] she made it a rule that students not be given anything in writing and should not be allowed to take notes or tape-record Reiki classes. This requirement prevented accurate records from being created about how she taught. Since her students had only memory to rely on, over time, changes developed in how Reiki was practiced and taught. In addition to variations in how her students remembered information, Takata sometimes changed what she taught from class to class.

All of this has created confusion within the Reiki community about the history and practice of Reiki and has allowed many conflicting ideas and systems to develop. Only through careful research, including interviews with her few surviving students and information from her two biographies has it been possible to discover how she did actually practice and teach. This information is provided in the previous article titled: *How Hawayo Takata Practiced and Taught Reiki.*

However, I recently learned that Takata didn't always teach the oral tradition. This fact came to me by the way of a packet I received in the mail from Alice Picking. Alice had taken a Reiki I class from Takata in June 1975 in Cherry Hill, New Jersey. In this class Takata mentioned nothing about an oral tradition. Instead, she provided instructional handouts to her students and allowed them to take notes. The packet I received included Alice's copy of the handouts Takata had given students, along with the notes she had taken. She also sent her Reiki certificate signed by Takata, several handwritten letters from Takata, along with a postmarked envelope, and the class list of 20 students. I talked with several of the students on the class list, and they verified the information Alice had sent me. In addition, a March 1975 newspaper article included at the end of this article validates that Alice had hosted Takata's class.

Page 105: Alice included several pages of class handouts Takata had given to her class. These include the one shown on page 105 and the next page, plus an additional page and a half of recipes. Her notes show that Takata taught only a few simple hand positions.

[2] After Takata's death, Takata's daughter, Alice Takata Furumoto, gave this manual to John Gray. See Gray's book, p. 183-195.

REIKI HEALING

Just for today: Thou shall not anger
Thou shall not worry
Thou shall count your blessings
Thou shall revere your parents, teachers, and friends
Thou shall earn an honest living
Thou shall be kind to all living things

REIKI brings health, happiness, security, and long life.

Religious people call this power cosmic energy.
Yoga defines it as prahna.
Hawaiian word is k[illegible]akilima - meaning medicine of the hands.
The people you are helping need not believe in what you are doing.

CAUSES OF ILLNESSES: Things that we eat
Our thoughts
Accidents

TREATMENT: Eliminate symptoms then go to the source of problem by using the basic positions.

BASIC POSITIONS: 1, 2, 3, 4, in front of body
1, 2, 3 in back of body

** There may be reactions to treatment. Worst can be slight fever and cold (or flu) symptoms. Keep treating.

Use basic positions for preventive, general health treatment.
Approximately 10-15 min each position.

For relazation in putting one to sleep: treat eyes, throat, just below voice box, positions 3 and 4 in front of body; about 5 min each.

For accidents, go directly to affected parts.

For illnesses, treat until symptom disappears or improvement seen. Go to cause and/or affected parts using the basic positions to find out cause.

Eyes - Treat eyes, temple, back of head.
For cross eyes, use exercise-trace a square with eyes.
For sties, also go to stomach, go to ovary for women.

Simus problems - Treat eyes but closer to nose bridge(pinch bridge), throat, and just below voice box.
Go to top of eyes for headaches just behind eyes.

Nose bleeding - Pinch nose bridge with one hand, other hand at nape of neck.

Minor nose bleeding -Use eye treatment plus just below ear lobe.

Diabetes - Treat pancreas.

Ear problems - Treat front and back of ears (for aches resulted from flu, measle, etc.)

Tooth ache -Treat outside cheek (with fillings, pain may return if fluid is not drained).

(2)

Tongue(cold sores) - Treat bottom of feet (near toes) and diet (too acid).

Sores on lips - Stomach too acid; treat affected area.

Tonsil - Direct

Throat - Direct; if symptom returns, treat solar plexus.
If there is phlegm, cut out diary products, take plenty of lemon juice (no sugar) and water?

Migraines - Women ovaries (liver condition)
Men Digestive system, too much good foods if pain occurs every night after dinner.
Other type - Treat liver(and testis (?))

Tension - Treat solar plexus.

For shock - Treat adrenal gland
For Hemorrhoid - Treat tail bone (prostate gland)

Nervous Breakdown - 10 inches from left shoulder in back of body.

Gall stone -Treat front(basic positions), then 10 inches from right shoulder.

Rheumatism×Bursitis - Treat kidney and affected part; take plenty of lenom juice(no sug

Small of back (usually from labor for women) - Basic positions and back(plus ovary for women).

For proper elimination - Treat kidney.

Eczema (weep skin rash) - Caused when your garbage can(stomach) gets too full.

Goiter(enlarged thyroid) - caused by ovarian treble. By the time it shows up, it is chronic, but it will go down in 20-30 treatments.

For fever, ovaries (cramps or pain) - Treat chest.

*****

Lecithin - good for brains.
Peanut shell tea - good for diabetes(in addition to Reiki). Pour boiling water over peanut shells. Let steep, and then drink the tea.

For quick pick up - grapefruit juice, raw egg, 1/2 cup water. Whir in blender.
For general good health - soy bean milk. Soak soy beans overnight(1 cup of beans), blend with 4 cups of water. Drink for breakfast.

For washing system out - 1/2 lemon to 10 ounces of water, without sugar.
Hawayo's salad - eat a cup of this before dinner; it also makes you eat less.
Cabbage, cauliflour, raw peeled beet, 1 apple. Grate the ingredients, Don't chop. Mix with a little mayonaise/ketchup and garlic salt. Mix with Reiki hands to give it ENERGY.
Another good rejuvenating fluid - Watercress, cabbage, celery, beet juice-blend with blender.

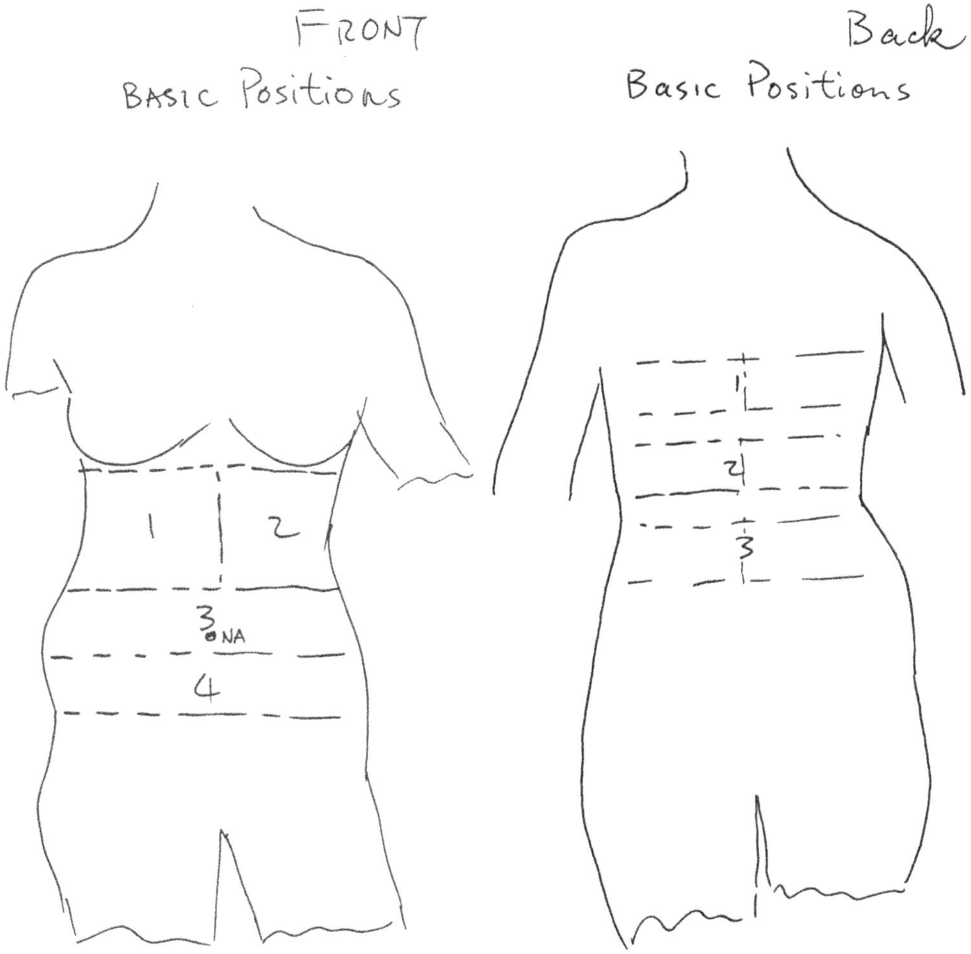
FRONT
BASIC Positions
1
2
3
NA
4
Back
Basic Positions
1
2
3

Seasons Greetings for a Happy Prosperous 1977.

I wish to thank you all for the many kindness given me, with gifts, bouquets, invitations to your lovely homes to share the feasts you so kindly prepared with Love and Reiki Hands.

It is with gratitude and Aloha to you all, that I write this letter to say "Thank You," to let you know that time has come for me to retire this year. I have gained many friends and students during my Reiki Tours, these past years. They were a great Joy, Inspiring receiving knowledge and Wisdom.

Wishing you the Best of Health, Happiness, to have Security and prepare for Longevity, Peace of mind and Success!!!

I remain, most gratefully yours,

Rev. Hawayo Takata

I have created 3 Reiki Masters to carry on this noble work. They are trusting, capable, kind and with humility serve God and mankind. They are :–

Master John Gray

Master Virginia Samdahl

Master Ethel Lombardi

Addresses and phone numbers have been removed to protect privacy

Above: Takata Letter from 1977. Included in the packet from Alice Picking was a letter Takata sent out to those who sponsored her classes. In it Takata thanks all who helped her promote Reiki and states she will be retiring. Added at the end is the statement that she has created three Reiki Masters to "carry on this noble work." This is important because it indicates that she didn't appoint these three to be Grandmasters who would be in charge of Reiki, nor that they would be her successors in any official capacity, but that their purpose was simply to carry on the work of Reiki.[3] Apparently she changed her mind about retiring and about having only three Masters. She created many more (a total of 22) and continued to practice and teach until her passing at the end of 1980.

Alice Pickering Hosts Mrs. Takata's Class: The below article provides additional evidence that Alice Pickering was a host of Mrs. Takata's class. It is from *The Forum*, a Hackettstown, New Jersey newspaper dated Wednesday, March 19, 1975.

Seminar Is Planned At Panther Valley

Area adherents of "Creative Consciousness," a program teaching participants how to make the most of their individual potential, have announced plans for a New Jersey seminar in the program April 4-6 at the Panther Valley Conference Center near Allamuchy.

Registration at the conference center, on Route 519 just off the Interstate Route 80 interchange at Allamuchy, will be at 5:30 p.m. April 4. Sessions will be held from 6 p.m. until midnight April 4 and from 9 a.m. to 9 p.m. April 5 and 6.

An introductory presentation on Creative Consciousness will be held at the Howard Johnson Motor Lodge on Route 22, Phillipsburg, from 2 to 4 p.m. March 22.

According to the program's literature, it teaches techniques to maximize mental productivity, improves memory, increases problem-solving potential and ability to make quick decisions, releases a person's creative ability, helps in communication with others and develops proper relaxation.

The group also plans sponsorship of two classes in Reiki healing by Mrs. Hawayo Takata of Hawaii in June.

Classes will be held June 1-4 at the home of Nick Siderides at 20 Brookdale Court in Cherry Hill and June 5-8 at the home of Jean Perry, Jane's Chapel Road, Oxford R.D.

Each class will be limited to 30 and will be open to the public but priority will be given to Creative Consciousness graduates if more than 30 persons apply for each class.

The hosts for the classes or Mrs. Alice Picking of Jane's Chapel Road, Oxford, one of the two New Jersey coordinators for Creative Consciousness, may be contacted for registration.

There is a fee of $125.

Mrs. Takta, who is 74, is Hawaii's only Reiki master, learning the healing art in 1935 in Japan after it had been applied successfully in treatment of her problems with asthma in 1935. She has practiced Reiki in Hawaii 39 years with clients who have included Barbara Hutton and Doris Duke.

According to Mrs. Takata, Reiki "helps attain health, happiness and security which leads to the road of longevity". She says the method, applied with the hands, uses cosmic energy to heal the ill and that "an unseen spiritual power radiates vibrations and lifts one into harmony."

In an interview in Hawaii, she said she believes a dynamic force from the divine spirit governs the world and the universe and is available to anyone interested in learning the art of healing.

Mrs. Takata, who said she has played golf every morning for 30 days, lectures at the University of Hawaii, is writing a book and hopes to build a Reiki center on land she owns in Olaa, near Kurtistown in Hawaii.

3 The concept of Grandmaster of Reiki didn't develop until after Takata passed. Soon after her passing, Barbara Weber Ray, one of the 22 Masters, declared that Takata had appointed her as Grandmaster of Reiki. This title was not a part of the Usui system, and Ray offered no meaningful proof to support her claim. Shortly after this, a group of Takata's Masters asked Phyllis Furumoto if she would be the Grandmaster, and she accepted. Because there was little authentic historical information about Reiki at this time, many people accepted the concept of Grandmaster, but as research revealed the facts, this idea lost credibility within the Reiki community.

Reiki in Japan

After Usui Sensei's transition in 1926, the practice of Reiki was preserved by the organization he started: the Usui Reiki Ryoho Gakkai. However, after World War II, strict laws were passed about healing that required one to have a massage or medical license to practice Reiki. Rather than conform to this requirement the Gakkai decided to continue as a secret organization. They stopped giving public lectures and advertising, and the members talked about Reiki only among themselves. They would admit new members to join their group and study Reiki only as replacements for members who died. Once one became a Shinpiden or Master, he or she wasn't allowed to teach or even talk about Reiki outside the Gakkai. They also had strict rules governing who was allowed to be a member Because of this, it was very difficult for anyone to find out anything about Reiki in Japan after World War II and almost impossible to learn it. The Usui Reiki Ryoho Gakkai remains a secret organization even today, and no one outside of the Gakkai is giving the same attunement that Usui Sensei gave.

As a result of this secrecy, Takata became the main source for training and information about Reiki from 1940 until the early 1990's. Those in Japan who wanted to learn Reiki turned to Western Takata-style teachers who traveled to Japan to teach, or they took classes in the USA. Reiki sessions have been exchanged between Gakkai members and those from the Takata lineage, and these sessions indicate that both styles seem to provide a similar level of healing ability. Tadao Yamaguchi, who learned from his mother, Chiyoko, teaches a Reiki style whose lineage goes directly to Hayashi Sensei and attempts to closely follow his teaching. However, most Reiki teachers in Japan today are teaching a combination of Japanese and Takata-style Reiki.

My Background and the History of the International Center for Reiki Training

BY WILLIAM LEE RAND

I LEARNED REIKI I on the Big Island of Hawaii in 1981 from Bethel Phaigh, who had learned from Mrs. Takata. In 1982, I received Reiki II from Bethel. I loved Reiki and started a Reiki practice. Because of the high fee for Reiki Master training and other restrictive rules, I did not think that becoming a Reiki Master was part of my spiritual path. However, Reiki has a way of guiding us in the way we should go, and through a number of coincidences and fortunate circumstances I met Diane McCumber in 1989. She was a Reiki Master of the Takata/Ishikura lineage and was charging a very reasonable fee to train Reiki Masters. I took her training and began to teach.

I chose to allow the Reiki energy to guide how I would teach. Rather than adhere strictly to the rules set by Takata Sensei, I wanted to do everything I could to help my students learn Reiki and use it in a way that was right for them. If they wanted to start a Reiki practice or to teach, then I wanted them to be as successful as possible.

To further this purpose, I took everything I had learned about Reiki to that point, organized the information and placed it in a class workbook that included drawings of the Reiki hand positions, which I then gave to my Reiki students. I began to research the history of Reiki seeking to verify the ideas that were taught and to discover the evidence based facts about the practice of Reiki. With information derived in this way, I have continued to expand and update the workbook as I have learned more about Reiki and its practice.

From the beginning, I encouraged students to take notes and to tape record the classes; I openly answered all questions and actively encouraged my students to do well. I taught the value of developing one's intuition and having confidence in one's experience and personal decision-making abilities. Knowing that one can always learn more I continued to study with other teachers and eventually took the Master Training from five additional Masters including three from Japan. This added to my understanding of Reiki as each teacher had gained many unique insights about how Reiki works and how to practice it. This helped me begin to understand the essence of Reiki and to learn how to allow it to more clearly guide my path.

I make it a point to acknowledge the value of other teachers and practitioners. In my travels, I continue to exchange Reiki information with them, looking for new information to use and pass on to others. Because I based my Reiki practice on the process of working in harmony with the qualities and values apparent in Reiki energy and following Reiki's guidance in carrying out my plans, my classes were always filled with students right from the beginning.

A newsletter was started in 1990 that continued to grow in size and readership and in 2002 became the *Reiki News Magazine*.

Wanting to maintain high standards for Reiki, I started a teacher certification program (now called our *Licensed Reiki Master Teacher* program that required additional training and takes three years to complete.

In 1995 we designed a website (www.reiki.org) that offers currently offers 1000 web pages with over 400 free articles on Reiki and many resources for those wanting to practice or teach. We also have a web store, which offers class workbooks, Reiki tables, and other products helpful to Reiki practitioners and teachers. (www.reikiwebstore.com)

In 1989, the Usui/Tibetan system of Reiki was created. Karuna Reiki® was developed in 1994 and Holy Fire Reiki was introduced in 2014. (www.reiki.org/holyfire.html).

We began the *Center for Reiki Research* in 2009 (www.centerforreikiresearch.org). Staffed by seven Ph.D qualified researchers, it contains references and summaries of all Reiki research studies published in peer-reviewed journals, a list of 70 hospital Reiki programs, and many useful articles and other features to help those interested in promoting an evidence-based understanding of Reiki. We've also started our own research study on pain in orthopedic patients due to be completed in 2014 and will expand this study into a large scale study due to begin in 2015.

In 2010, we created a professional Reiki Membership Association (www.reikimembership.com). The current membership of over 2400 Reiki practitioners and teachers offers Reiki sessions and classes across the U.S. and in some foreign countries.

I am grateful to all those who have gone before us and worked to establish the practice of Reiki and preserve its use. I am also thankful for the healing that so many receive and the wonderful feelings of joy, peace and love that Reiki provides for us to enjoy. I hope you have found the articles in this book to be informative and that they will help you to more fully experience the essence of Reiki in everything you do.

Made in United States
North Haven, CT
27 April 2024

51826982R00063